Catharine Gendron Poyas

Year of Grief and Other Poems

Catharine Gendron Poyas

Year of Grief and Other Poems

ISBN/EAN: 9783337779283

Printed in Europe, USA, Canada, Australia, Japan

Cover: Foto ©Thomas Meinert / pixelio.de

More available books at **www.hansebooks.com**

YEAR OF GRIEF,

And Other Poems,

BY

CATHARINE GENDRON POYAS.

CHARLESTON, S. C.:
WALKER, EVANS & COGSWELL, PRINTERS,
No. 3 Broad street.
1869.

CONTENTS

OF

PART THE FIRST.

CONTENTS

OF

PART THE SECOND.

PATRIOTIC.

CONTENTS

OF

PART THE THIRD.

PART THE FIRST.

Year of Grief, and other Poems.

'Tis sweet, as year by year we lose
Friends out of sight, in faith to muse
  How grows in Paradise our store.

Then pass, ye mourners, cheerly on,
  Through prayer unto the tomb,
Still as ye watch life's falling leaf,
Gathering from every loss and grief
  Hope of new spring and endless home.
                  ⌈KEBLE.

THE CHRISTMAS TREE.

AN ODE.

HAIL! O hail! bright Christmas Tree,
Type of Love and social glee!
Gladly hail! Thy branches green
Waving o'er our festive scene,
(Now the Jubilee of peace
Fills our hearts with fresh increase
Of domestic joys and pleasures,
And Religion's richer treasures)—
Bring remembrance of the hour
When on earth the fairest flower
That e'er bloomed in garden bright
Oped its petals to the light;
When the smile of Sharon's Rose
Did a Heavenly joy disclose;
And the Lily of the Vale
Breathed its odor to the gale:
Then when love to God and man
Through th' Eternal arches ran,
And waves of rich harmonious song
Floated the blue Heavens along;
While a glad Angelic train
Hovered o'er Judea's plain,
On th' astonished shepherd's sight,
Bursting in a vision bright,

While from every golden string
Of their gemméd harps they fling
Sounds seraphic—the blue air
Vibrates to their voices clear,
Chanting to the earth and sky,
" Glory to God, enthronéd high,
" Love on earth to men of love,
" And peace soft nestling as a dove !"—
Hark ! the echo of the strain
Dies along Judea's plain.—
But the church in every land
Loves to join the cherub band,
And as year by year speeds round
Swells the song on holy ground ;
See her temples richly dight
With green leaves and berries bright !
And shall we no poems sing ?
No hosannas to our King ?
Shall we no thank-offerings bear
To the Virgin-born, the heir
Of all things above—below,
Spring whence all our blessings flow !
Have we no rich garbs to vie
With the robes of Tyrian dye
In His pathway to outspread ?
No bright garland for the head
Of the Prince of Peace ?   Behold !
No rare spices, gems or gold
Have we, for the royal stranger
Cradled in the lowly manger,
But we dedicate our tree,
God of Peace and Love, to Thee !
Thou who our fair lot hast set

In a goodly country, wet
With the kindly dews of grace,
Where the smile of Heaven we trace
In the blessings that abound;
In the fruitage of the ground.
Thou who makest us to dwell,
Bound by Love's divinest spell—
In fair Orbs or Circlets trine,
That appear *as one* to shine;
God of the Christian's home and hearth,
Deign to bless our pious mirth!

Thus devoted, now our rite
We renew with glad delight—
Banished now be every feeling
O'er our evil natures stealing;
Let each emulous desire
From our bosoms far retire;
Let each envious demon fly,
Joy illumine every eye;
Bid each jealous sprite depart,
Love alone fill every heart!

Hail our Christmas Tree! And now
Yield thy fruit from branch and bough.

Here our aged matrons find
Fruitage to delight their mind,
Ripened by affection's ray,
Glittering with the dewy spray
Shed from eyes that love them best
As their star towards the west
Sinks—to rise with brighter ray
In regions of Eternal Day!

Here our fathers and each spouse
May from thy prolific boughs
Gather fruits that never cloy—
Fruits of pure domestic joy;
For the branch that doth them bear
Was in Eden plucked—and here
Well ingrafted—ere that bower
Fell 'neath Satan's baneful power!

Here the lonely-hearted find
Leaflets of a healing kind,
To assuage the pains that dwell
In their bosoms' deepest cell.

Youth and Maidens, standing fair
On the threshold of Hope's year,
Here are buds of Love for you
Sparkling in affection's dew!

Children! lovely flowers that spring
All about our paths, and fling
Such strong tendrils 'round the heart—
Come and bear away your part
From our richly ladened Tree;
Come—advance in merry glee—
E'en our darling baby boy
Here will find his plum of joy,
And stretch his little arms in pleasure
To seize upon the tempting treasure!

Thus our pleasant rite is ended,
In which Love and Duty blended.
Naught remains but that our prayer
Rise for ancient Limerick—dear

To each heart within her gate ;
Health and honor on her wait !
On each happy Christmas tide
May green branches, fair and wide,
Their rich fruitage on her shed,
And wave above her honored head.

Christmas, 1851.

ۤear of Grief—1852.

"WEEP NOT."

I.

How slight a stroke can ope the cave of Thought,
    And send its waters gushing o'er the soul,
    Where late sterility held full control,
Soft'ning its fallow.   Now to light are brought
The flowers of Poesie and Love, inwrought
    With the rich gems of Fancy.   At the gaol
    Of that bright streamlet, Hope the glittering pole
Of his gay banner rears ; Its folds are caught
By the glad air and flutter on her breast.
    And such a gentle touch my spirit's cell *
Received of late, from one beyond the crest
    Of blue Atlantic wave.   His wizard spell,
And wand enchanted, stirred the quiet nest
    And woke the bird its tender notes to swell.

---

* Rev. Isaac Williams of England.

II.

How strange that I unknowing and unknown,
　　Filling my little nook so far away,
　　Where summer suns with burning radiance play
O'er fields of golden rice—where winter's throne
Is garlanded with flowers—and his zone
　　Studded with sparkling gems—whose robes display
　　The emerald tint of nature ; That I may
For friend of mine a noble poet own !
　　One whose deep thoughts have moved the world I
　　ween,
　　(From where of royal blood, the British Queen
Holdeth her loving state—to where the sea
Laves with green flood the Nation of the Free)—
　　Causing all faithful souls to bow the knee
To Jesus, in His Church and gospel seen.

III.

Yet is it thus: And his resounding lyre
　　Hath moved the slumbering chords within my mind ;
　　My thoughts heave up, as when a mighty wind
Tosses the sea ; my soul is all on fire,
And my heart throbs with its intense desire
　　To sweep once more the strings ! No rest I find
　　For its perturbed throes. No power to bind
Calm trust to yon pale star should me inspire
To hymn the fallen year. A season dark—
　　Replete with sorrows to the Church and State ;
That quenched in many a soul the vital spark,
　　And sent them darkling to the gloomy gate
Of shadowy Hades ; where in hope or fear,
They wait the dawn of the Eternal Year.

IV.

O dismal cycle of distress and pain—
   When Death hath marched along in awful state
   Sweeping towards Eternity! Where late
As flowerets smiling on a sunny plain,
Or fruitful fields of wavy golden grain,
   Our dear ones bloomed around us—Cruel Fate
   Led on the train of Death, and desolate
Our pleasant homes and loving hearts remain.
No more shall we our cherished friends behold!
   No more infold them in our warm embrace;
No more enjoy the pleasures manifold
   Springing from sweet communion; with them trace
The footprints of the Shepherd of the fold,
   Where rest the flock beneath His smile of Grace.

V.

It dawned in gladness, the deceitful year—
   We hailed its coming with a merry chime
   Of heartfelt music, for the Christmas time
And the Old Year, floating to meet the clear,
Fresh day-spring of the New. Sorrow's sad tear
   Soon fell to damp the music—or sublime
   Its notes to strains cherubic! Wintry rime
Flung its cold shroud, all glittering and fair,
O'er our most tender plant. The gentle child*
   Bowed his meek head upon his mother's arm,
And his blue eyes, so beautifully mild,
   Closed for their long, long slumber; No alarm
Felt he at Death's approach—but sweetly smiled,
Clothed in baptismal vesture undefiled.

---

* M. G. B. died January 26th, 1852, aged 15 months.

VI.

Angel unsullied—from thy flower-strown bier
  I culled a violet and safely prest
  Between my Bible leaves—a place of rest
Meet for the lovely token.   It is there
Where with prophetic glance the holy seer
  Viewed the meek infant on his mother's breast,
  Alas! to be yet torn from that calm nest,
And stretched on bloody rood, His death-bed drear—
As day by day the sacred leaves I turn
  I see it shorn of beauty—but my heart
Inshrines its essence in its golden urn :
  O may its sweetness to my life impart
A perfume not of earth—until I yearn
For the bright realm where richest odors burn !

VII.

Again an angel's blissful voice I hear !
  For only yesterday another gem,
  Plucked from the modest violet's quivering stem
Springing above a grave,* a mourner there
With trembling hand confided to my care.
  And does that earthen cavern now inhem
  A precious jewel, in the diadem
Of Jesus yet to blaze !   In accents clear
This solemn truth the voice of Wisdom cries,
  " The graves shall ope—the sea give up the dead."
Hark ! through the vaults of Heaven the echo flies—
  Angels in wonder list the awful tread
Of the approaching judgment—and their eyes
  Look for the dawning of that Day of dread.

---

* The grave of F. G. B., a lovely babe, who died after a long illness,
September, 1850.

VIII.

Then thou, our beautiful! away shalt dart
  On wing of brightness soaring, to abide
  Forever with the Saviour's glorious bride,
A gentle dove nestled upon her heart.
Whilst here on Earth thou hadst thy tragic part—
  To play on thy small stage. By Jesus' side
  Stretched on thy cross of agony, the tide
Of thy short life ebbed out, 'mid cruel smart
Caused by the serpent's sting. But long before
Religion on the parents' hearts could pour
  The balm of healing, at the crystal gate
  Of Paradise, thy ransomed soul elate
Sung its glad song of triumph, as of yore
The angels at primeval Eden's door!

IX.

Hark to the voice of wailing! Deep the woe
  Of our beloved Sion. On the ground
  In her sad widowhood, her locks unbound,
She sits forlorn in sorrow. For her flow
Her children's bitter tears—and bending low,
  Her Priests her sacred Altars now surround
  Wrapped in deep grief and agony profound.
What bodes this solemn, dim, funereal show?—
The Angel of God's Temple ta'en away; *
  Vicegerent here below of Jesus dead—
  Her spouse, her master. Therefore is her head
Bowed as a bulrush, and her tresses grey
Loose in the wintry winds disordered play:—
  Our Mother must the bitter wine-press tread.

---

* Bishop C. E. Gadsden died St. John Baptist's day, June 24th, 1852.

X.

Prone in the dust the crown and crosier lie ;
   The Apostolic vestments on the throne
   Rest all untenanted.   Our Bishop gone
To render up his stewardship to the High
Omniscient Judge of mortals.   Sion's sigh
   Reëchoes through her arches, and a moan,
   As of departed spirits hither borne
From their deep caves oblivious makes reply.
Dark the funereal banners float above
   The Altar of his rest.   Meek Overseer,
And Shepherd of the flock!   High Priest of Love!
   Shall we no more behold thy visage here,
Beaming with all the graces of the Dove
   From thy Episcopate's exalted sphere?

XI.

On whom shall thy descending mantle rest?
   Who is there strong enough to bear the weight
   And care of all the churches?   Brave the hate
Of Hydra-headed schism?   On his breast
Wear manfully the Spirit's shield imprest?
   And clad in the Heavenly armor never bate
   In holy zeal, though foes assail the gate
And ancient walls of Sion?   When distressed
To bear her most in heart—and never quail
   Though ghostly foes against her bend their ire?—
O sainted Bishop! may *thy* prayers prevail,
   Floating as incense from thy heart of fire—
   Far, far above the bright angelic choir
To the Eternal One—beyond the veil!

XII.

O cruel stroke of agonizing fear!
  E'en as the lightning flash in summer time
  Breaks from a thunder cloud, with crash sublime
Filling all hearts with dread. So on our ear
Fell the sad news that thou wert ill, our dear,
  Our much loved brother! Thou the very prime,*
  And crown of our rejoicing! Hark! the chime
Of Sabbath bells invite us to draw near
Our Father's House: With bleeding hearts we go
Pouring the bitter torrents of our woe
  Before the Saviour's throne. His pitying eye
Sheds on the stream of sorrow in its flow
  A ray of Love Divine. All tremblingly
  To Him in every trial let us fly!

XIII.

Thine was a direful struggle—long and fierce,
  Along the darksome valley all must tread
  To reach the silent caverns of the dead:
Encountered on all sides by foes perverse,
The Spirit's weapon could alone disperse,
  And with it thou wert armed. As o'er thy head
  Gleamed the keen edge of Prayer—an awful dread
Filled their black hearts—with deeply muttered curse
All terror-struck they shrink amid the gloom.
And now in peaceful beauty for the tomb
  Our youthful brother lies. All dimmed the light,
Erst from his torch of life serenely bright,
  Enlightened far and near. O fearful blight,

---

* John Ball of Hyde Park, St. John's Berkley.

XIV.

When the pure-hearted perish in their bloom !
O how mysterious is the tragic fate,
   Did Husband, Father, Son and Brother tear
   From our fond arms and left us weeping here !
So many households rendered desolate :
May we thy shining virtues imitate !
   E'en when Death's gloomy torrent, wild and drear,
   Poured its harsh music on thy list'ning ear,
Thou didst thyself from terrors extricate,
And with a fearless spirit braved its tide,
And sought the Rock of Ages, there to bide
Safe in the sheltering clefts upon its side :
   O may we to the same sure refuge fly,
   Ere the thick film is settling on the eye ;
   Ere the cold breast has heaved its farewell sigh.

XV.

Ah ! yes ! the fearful agony is o'er—
   And cold in death our Brother's body lies,
   His soul departed to its native skies,
For he was pure in heart—and we are sure
Such shall on Heavenly Heights their God adore,
   And on his glory look with blissful eyes.
   O after his may our dull souls arise,
Mounting on hopeful pinions to the shore
Where sin and sorrow cease. E'en as at sea
   The stormy petrel rests his weary wing
Upon the heaving billow, so may we
Just pause upon the Ocean-swell of Life
To gather courage, for the onward strife
   Shall bring us to the mansion of our King.

XVI.

O who may paint the anguish of the hour
  That summoned us to meet around thy bier,
  And with heart-rending sob or silent tear
Consign thee to the grave—Death's fearful bower
Hid from the cheering sun and silent shower.
  Like to the faithful Mary, lone and drear
  Sat thy fond mother in the chapel—where
The burial rite resounded: Sad the dower
By Heaven appointed to her stricken heart.
There brothers, sisters, kindred bore their part
  In the sad scene of anguish. Friends around
  In tearful silence view the grief profound—
With the keen sorrow deeply sympathize
And give the balmy tribute of their sighs.

XVII.

" What means that fearful, wild, half-savage cry
  Filling the heart with horror and affright,
  Making day hideous as blackest night,
When boding owls spread their dark wings and fly
From the old tombs and hoary oak-trees nigh ?"
  Let those discordant sounds your souls excite
  To gentlest pity—thus th' untutored spright
Of Afric's sons their grief would testify
For a loved master's loss. Just such the strain
  Resounded through Machpelah's ancient cave
And died away in Hebron's flowery glade,
  When the old Patriarch to his rocky grave
Was borne in sad procession by his train
  Of faithful servants, and by Sarah laid !

XVIII.

Like some calm Reservoir within a wood,
   'Round which the gemmèd leaves of Autumn sigh,
   Reflecting Heaven within its azure eye
Rests thy sweet Relict in her widowhood.
Hid from the world in sylvan solitude,
   She lists the spirit-voices as they cry
   Their solemn warnings to the wintry sky;
Fit music for her sadly pensive mood.
Close to the margent of that placid lake,
   A little flower-bud from its grassy bed
Peeps forth with eye of Love. From out the brake
   The bird of Peace is singing. " Bow thy head,
   Pale mourner! where the Saviour's board is spread;
All thy heart-sorrows to His keeping take."

XIX.

Mother beloved! upon whose matron brow
   Serenely beautiful! Rich Autumn bound
   A garland of rare foliage—slowly wound
By Time's mysterious fingers. Altered now
And withered is its brightness. As the bough
   Of some fair evergreen is sadly found
   Torn by a blast and strown upon the ground,
Reft of its once high honors: Even so
This storm of grief has dealt with the rich crown,
   It lies in dust and ashes—in its place
   A hoar and blighted circle now we trace,
For Winter stern has marked thee as his own:
   Nor here again shall God renew thy bloom—
   But Spring immortal reigns beyond the tomb!

XX.

And thy beloved hath reached that happy shore ;
  Thy beautiful, thy pure and spotless boy—
  Bright as the angels now his crown of joy !
And though thine eye shall never greet him more
On this terrene.   Yet let thy soul adore
  The God of Judgment—and thy tongue employ
  To sing His praise who wrought this dread annoy :
He hath escaped the tempest's awful roar—
Lo ! 'mid the sacred host with footsteps free
  He walketh by the crystal river clear,
And plucks the healing leaflets from the tree
  Yielding in monthly cycles fruitage fair,
The Tree of Life !   O bow in awe the knee,
  For the pure throne of God's own Lamb is there !

XXI.

Yet still a golden chain doth bind thee here—
  One end is fastened to th' Eternal Throne,
  The other linked unto the kindly zone
Encircling thy fond heart—Thy offspring dear—
By it thy soul, as on a golden stair,
  Ascends from Earth to Heaven.   And thou must own,
Relict beloved ! not every comfort flown,
Bright rainbow tints are glowing in each tear—
Thy child—lone sporting on life's flowery lea
  To cull those flowers aright—'tis thine to teach ;
A fragile shell tossed on a wintry sea—
  'Tis thine to see he safely make the beach,
And with his brother gems forever be
  Set in a star of threefold brilliancy !

XXII.

Once more 'mid thy ancestral honors set,
　　Brother beloved! Why do our fond eyes trace
　　The lines of anguish furrowed on thy face?
Whilst ever and anon thy cheeks are wet
With sorrow's silent tear-drop? O not yet
　　May thy true heart expel the noble grace
　　Of thy loved brother's form. When for the chase
Thou windst thy bugle call, canst thou forget
How, like the morning star, serenely clear,
　　His smiling visage at the casement beamed
Radiant with hopeful pleasure! Never here
　　May thy fond glance rest on him. Vainly dreamed
Thy soul of joys fraternal—dry and sere
Their withered blossoms strew thy pathway drear.

XXIII.

Lone brother! sad indeed would be thy fate
　　But for a loving spirit in thine ear,
　　Whispering in silvery accents, soft and clear
As the wind-notes of even, "Thy loved mate
Seek not in slumber's chamber desolate,
　　Where their moss banners on the angry air
　　The hoary oak-boughs wave—He is not there—
His bright celestial home by Death's dark gate
His soul hath entered. In its Courts of Light
　　He walketh with the beatific train
　　Of God's elect. Their robes of spotless white,
Washed in the precious blood of Jesus slain,
　　Glow with seraphic radiance. Stars of night
Less brightly beam upon yon ebon plain."

XXIV.

Meek, unobtrusive grief—seeking to hide
  The shaft beneath the wing. The starting tear
  Lone witness to the anguish resting there.
Floating along on Duty's peaceful tide,
Sweet sorrowing sister! When thy looks abide
  On yonder cottage, snugly nestled where
  The crystal waters lave the fenny mere,
And golden shafts repose at even-tide—
Is not the light of Recollection thrown
  Full on another scene? A quiet nest,
Where a fond mother-bird, her partner flown,
  Warms her dear fledgling at her widowed breast,
Wounded, dispirited, afflicted, lone—
List'ning in heart, sweet Mercy's undertone.

XXV.

Another and another—thus I tell
  My rosary of sorrow; every bead
  A ruby drop from wounded hearts that bleed.
Nun-like retired in thy spirit's cell,
Thou commun'st with the loud, convulsive swell
  Of thy great grief—Sister in heart and deed
  To our beloved kinsman. But thy creed
Instructs thee where to turn when sorrows dwell
Deep in the soul. Building thy bower of Hope
Beneath the cross, the gale of peace shall ope
  Love's roses in thy breast, and glowing there
Within thy ardent bosom's pious scope
  Shall lend their perfume to the morning air,
  Their rosy petals moist with Memory's tear.

2

XXVI.

Spirit! o'er whom this storm of sorrow swept
  With twofold agony!   O I have borne
  On heart of love thy anguish to the throne
Of the Eternal Father, and there wept,
Whilst from their sullen caves the night Fiends crept.
  But now the angry blast hath overflown—
  And gentle showers succeed the dismal moan
Glowing with Hope's bright iris.   Duty slept—
But now awakes and strows Life's rugged road
With flowers of sweet content.   On thy abode
  Broodeth the bird of birds—the Holy Dove!
  Sheltered beneath his wings of Peace and Love
Mayest thou forever rest 'till care's sad load
  Change to "the weight of glory" there Above!

XXVII.

Youth, on whose sympathy and loving care
  Two widowed hearts repose; a weighty charge
  Might well the current of thy life enlarge
Till it o'erflow in Love.   The manly tear
Down-falling for thy Sister's orphan heir;
  And thine own orphaned household.—These surcharge
  Thy breast with anxious freight, till like a barge
Laden from Ind it founders with rich ware,
Wouldst thou thy precious cargo safely moor?
  Let thy keen glance the cresset beacon mark
  Far gleaming on th' horizon border dark,
  Bright as a star—then fading to a spark;
And as its fitful fires thus allure
Let the Great Chart thy onward course assure!

XXVIII.

Peace to thy heart, dear Mother—peace to thee!
  Methinks I see thee in thy cottage home
Plying thy task with busy industry
  From morn to night. Perchance a mighty tome
  Engrosses thy attention. Tales have come
Far down the track of ages. Or, I see
Thy spirit revelling 'neath antique tree
  Of some forgotten name! Thy humble dome
Thou wouldst not now exchange for palace grand,
  So happy in the dim, mysterious chase
Of ghostly forms along the shadowy-land.
  Thanks to the Mighty Friend, who thus doth brace
Thy every nerve for action; for a band
  Of leagued sorrows track thy lonely pace.

XXIX.

Cord of anxiety! of triple woof
  Stretching along my life—all dun of hue
  Saving that here and there a thread of blue,
Or Love's fine gold peeps out. Soul-cheering proof
That underneath the clear, cerulean roof
  Sheltering our home we cannot ever rue.
Love's buds are always sprinkled with soft dew
Falling from Heaven! though some time calm reproof
Looks with paternal eye from out a cloud.
  O heart of mine, weave garlands of bright Hope
Upon the tightened cord—and pierce the shroud
  With the keen eye of Faith. Then God shall ope
For thee a door of gladness, whence the loud
  Hosannah shall ring out from Heaven's high cope.

XXX.

Sisters, in whose domestic arbors grow
   The flowers that deck my lone, sequestered cell,
   O where shall I find words of power to tell
The deep, mysterious, silent, endless flow
Of love, from cave where gems immortal glow
   For you and yours—that dark unfathomed well
   My throbbing heart! And now with grateful swell
My soul I lift that this sad year of woe
Left you unscathed. No storm of sorrow flung
   Its darksome veil above your pleasant bowers,
Save that the shadow of the banner hung
   By Death's dark hand upon our triple towers
Eclipsed their light. And sighs of anguish rung
   Your hearts responsive to the grief of ours!

XXXI.

Ah! some upon whose cheek the sorrowing tear
   For us was scarcely dry, are called to weep
   O'er their own anguish, cruel, sore and deep;
A first-born son cut down in manhood's year—
Sad trial for paternal hearts to bear!—
   But O, more sad—more dreadful is the sweep
   Of agony across that soul, must keep,
All lonely now her watch and vigil drear!
O cousin mine! stern was thy fate exiled
   From home and kindred ties. But one was found,
One faithful heart to cheer the rugged wild:
   She with a wreath of Love thy spirit bound
To simple joys domestic. When she smiled
   Hope, in thy cottage, danced her cheerful round.

XXXII.

Once more from solemn tower the sonorous bell *
  Sends out its knell funereal. At the sound
  Bleedeth afresh the rude and ghastly wound
Deep in our Mother's side. Yea, that sad knell
Speaks of another spirit gone to dwell
  On the mysterious shore. A pastor found
  Faithful in word and deed hath passed the bound
Dividing Earth and Heaven. Freed from its shell
His spirit soared exulting to the sky.
  O blessed Saviour! wherefore lay thy hand
So rudely on thy Bride? Wouldst verify
  Her holy faith unto a reckless band
  Of unbelievers in this godless land—
Showing Religion's perfect purity?

XXXIII.

"O lay me not within the chancel bound: †
  Nor in the echoing aisles where footsteps ply;
  But lay me 'neath the calm, ethereal eye
Of th' o'er-arching firmament. The mound
Heap, where the clouds of Heaven may moist the ground
  With silvery tear-drops; there let violets shy
  Give out their perfume to the passer by,
Wafting his soul to God's celestial Round!
Place not thy Pastor in metallic shrine,
  But in a simple case may soon decay,
That so this perishable form of mine
  May mingle 'dust to dust' some early day,
Waiting the summons of the voice Divine—
  Then spring to life and hail th' eternal Ray!"

---

* Rev. Mr. Young, Rector of St. Michael's, Charleston.
† Mr. Young's dying request.

XXXIV.

And thou, ‡ within whose bosom now abode
   A two-edged sword of anguish, help to lay
   Thy Brother in the cold sepulchral clay
E'en as he wished.   And now Life's checkered road
To thee seems doubly rugged—and the load
   Of care weighs heavily, no cheering ray,
   From eye of Guide or Friend, to light thy way.
The rankling wound would thy sad heart corrode,
   But that as one by one thy loved ones die
   I see thee to the cross uplift thine eye,
   And bosom heaving with deep agony;
Thence blood of very God for sinners shed,
Drops as the dew upon thy drooping head,
Healing the wounds which else had festering spread.

XXXV.

One more funereal garland have I wound
   Of gloomy cypress; 'tis for yonder grave
Where rest the mortal members of a slave ‖
Honored, beloved, respected: Faithful found,
Walking with steady step his daily round
   Doing his Master's service.   He who gave
   Hath called him home across the dismal wave,
And his dark, thoughtful brow with glory crowned!
O remnant of the faithful ones of yore—
Shall we behold thy reverend form no more?
   We miss thee at the quiet hour of prayer
When, with the household band we God adore;
   Miss thee on Sabbath night when *all* draw near,
Owner and serf—one Master to implore.

---

‡ Rev. Cranmore Wallace, the Author's Pastor.
‖ Joe Bailey, of "Limerick," St. John's Berkley.

XXXVI.

All through the summer time, along our path
　　The fever fiend his burning torch waved high ;
　　Now o'er the cloud in-wrapped and wintry sky
The pestilence is sweeping in his wrath,
Armed with his gleaming sword.　May He who hath
　　Sent these stern ills His people's faith to try
　　Look from His Throne of Love with pitying eye
Upon our deep distress.　Increase our faith
In his all-wise appointments ; make us know
　　Himself the source of joy—the source of woe ;—
　　Then even should dark sorrow's cup o'erflow
With bitter draught of anguish, we shall feel
'Tis by a kind Physician sent to heal,
And drink it whilst in silent awe we kneel!

XXXVII.

Once more upon the mountain, hark ! the sound
　　Of old time-honored Christmas.　Haste to meet
　　And welcome to your bosom's warm retreat.
Alas ! no longer at the tidings bound
Our joyous hearts to greet him.　Tears have drowned
　　The rose of gladness.　Once our hearts quick beat
　　Respondent to the music of his feet—
Borne on the soft night wind.　But now the wound
In our bereaved bosoms cannot bear
　　His glad, bright eye of mirth.　Nay, bring him home,
He is a kind Physician—and a tear
　　Hath for the stricken ones beneath the dome
Of sorrow sighing.　To his healing care
Commit thy woe—he bringeth Jesus near—

XXXVIII.

The Prince of Peace! Even as on the morn
　　When the glad shepherds hastened o'er the plain
　　To welcome in Messiah's tranquil reign,
So peace, with him, shall on our bosoms dawn.
O feel we not our hearts resistless drawn
　　To meet him—heralding the happy train
　　Of Christian virtues. Ever to remain
Domestic here on earth? O who would pawn
For transitory pleasure, Heavenly. Grace?
　　Then let us hasten, and the Holy Child
Receiving from his arms with pure embrace
　　Cradle upon our bosoms, reconciled
　　To woe and sorrow. Then the radiance mild
Of Bethlehem's Star shall every grief efface.

XXXIX.

Wrapped in a mantle of deep gloom, the year
　　Is taking its departure. Slow his tread
　　As one who walketh 'mid the silent dead
In some lone church-yard. The pale sun draws near
His mansion in the western realms of air;
　　But not on couch of purple, gold and red
　　Shall rest to-night his proudly regal head—
A pilgrim grey he sinks upon yon drear
And dismal bank of clouds. With him doth fly
　　The stern Old Year, bearing his awful scroll
Before the Throne of Judgment, where the Eye
　　Of God shall scan the record. And each soul,
　　For weal or woe, within His Book enroll,
Till the slain Lamb reveal our Destiny!

XL.

For He alone is worthy found to break
  The sevenfold signet of the Book of Doom,
  On that dread morning when from yawning tomb
And hoary deep the startled dead shall wake,
And 'round the pure white Throne of Judgment take
  In silent awe their stand.   With hopeful plume,
  Or wing despondent shall each soul resume
Its dwelling in the flesh.   When Thou shalt make
Thine angels from the just the bad divide
  May we be found rejoicing—we who weep,
  And those who have already fallen asleep
In Jesus; and with palms triumphant glide
  In glad procession up the mountain steep
Into the pearly portals with Thy Bride!

NOTE.—These Sonnets form a continuous poem.

On the Death of the Right Rev. Christopher Edwards Gadsden, D. D.

" Blessed are the dead who die in the Lord, from henceforth ; Even
  so saith the Spirit, for they rest from their labors."

Our blessed dead—we've laid thee down
  To rest in holy ground,
Within the Temple of thy God ;
  Within the chancel bound :
Within the chancel's sacred rail,
  Beneath the Altar's shade,
With heavy hearts and streaming eyes,
  Thy sepulchre we've made.
3

Where should our holy Bishop rest
    But where he loved to be?
Fast by the altar of his God,
    Clothed with humility:
Not there to fill with robes of state
    The Apostolic chair,
But prostrate on its sacred steps
    To bow in earnest prayer.

O, what a flood of care would then
    O'er his meek spirit sweep!
What wonder he was fain to fall
    Prone in the dust and weep!
Care for the Church—care for her Priests—
    Care for her Deacon band;
The clergy—to their solemn task
    Appointed by his hand.

Care for his well-belovéd ones,
    His own peculiar sphere,
The flock o'er whom the Holy Ghost
    Had made him overseer;
The flock for whom for forty years
    He blessed the bread and wine—
How meet to lay your sainted Priest
    Within you holy shrine!

Care for the little lambs who loved
    To catch his pleasant smile,
What time the evening shadows fell
    Across each solemn aisle—
While they, a wreath of living flowers,
    Around the chancel clung,
Listening the blessed truths that fell
    So gently from his tongue.

Care for the sable race of Ham,
  The bondman and the free,
He scorned not in their humble homes
  To bend in prayer the knee!
Where'er a suffering member wept—
  A contrite sinner sighed;
Where'er was sorrow to be cured,
  A tear-drop to be dried;

There, like his Master, he was found
  Meek, sympathizing, kind;
Ready the hungry poor to feed,
  The broken spirit bind:
O surely on the Day of Doom
  That Master's voice shall cry,
"Enter, thou blessed of the Lord,
  The portals of the sky."

But ye for whom his yearning soul
  Has agonized in prayer,
Well may ye sigh your sorrows forth,
  Or drop the mournful tear;
And as ye bend your stricken forms
  Repentant 'neath the rod,
Bear up upon your troubled hearts,
  His household unto God.

O not in selfish, lonely grief
  Let sorrow's tide o'erflow,
Bear up the church upon your hearts—
  Full is her cup of woe!
Bear her upon your heart of hearts
  Before the Mercy Seat;
Bear her in love before her God,
  "'Tis bounden, right and meet."

But oh! not for our sainted one
  Be sigh or tear-drop given,
He walks among the blessed dead,
  A ransomed heir of Heaven;
His ear has heard—his eye has seen—
  His heart now comprehends,
A portion of the joy prepared
  For Jesus' loving friends.

Then leave him to his deep repose
  Beneath the altar's shade,
Assured his soul as calmly rests
  In Eden's blissful glade;
There, with th' innumerable host
  Of God's elect, erewhile
He waits th' Archangel's thrilling trump,
  Cheered by his Saviour's smile.

July, 1852.

A Voice of Wailing.

I WAS not here when thou wert laid to rest,
Within this silent chamber; was not here
When loving hands let thee so gently down
Within the bosom of God's holy earth
To sleep until the Judgment; and great drops
Fell fast from many eyes, unused to tears.
Not here when the vast throng of human souls,
That filled this sacred edifice, sent up,
As with one voice, a cry of wail to Heaven.
Alas! not here, the one who loved thee best,

Save her, who was to thee as thine own soul,
To mingle my deep grief with all who mourned;
The rich, the great, the needy, the unknown,
The doubly-orphaned children of The Home!
With contrite Magdalenes—and men once seen
In lowest haunts of vice—till led by thee
To wash them clean in blood of Jesus slain.

Who now, when pestilence walks forth at noon
Beneath the summer's sun; or the keen blasts
Of winter cause the poor of Christ to cry
To God in anguish, parched by fever heat,
Or numbed with deadly cold—shall dauntless go
To minister untiring to their wants,
All for the Saviour's sake? The willing mind
Victorious o'er the body racked with pain,
And often far too feeble for the work.
Then worn with toil, but *now* at perfect rest—
Not only in the grave where sure decay
Crumbles his silent form to kindred dust,
But in the peaceful regions of repose
Where spirits on the bosom of their God
Await in blissful hope, the perfect day,
When souls and bodies glorified in Christ,
Shall shine as stars in firmament of Heaven.

Witness, ye poor, who loved to hear his step
Upon the threshold, when pale Death was there
Busy amongst your dear ones; and Decay
Scarce waited for the darkness of the grave!—
Ye sick and aged! who from month to month,
Received the sacred alms from his kind hand,
And heard his voice beside your bed in prayer,
Ye souls reclaimed from vice! Ye stalwart men,

And feeble women whom he lifted up;
All witness if my praise exceed his meed,
Whose footsteps followed, humbly, those of Christ.

O come up to the rescue, men of God!
Fill up this breach in Sion—for a great
And mighty Captain hath been stricken down;
One, who with thoughtful brow and Eagle eye
Looked from her ramparts, and the deadly foe
Marked as he set his battle in array
Against the hosts of Israel; and the shock
Met firmly, clad in panoply divine.

Yea, hasten to the rescue—great the need—
For piteous is the cry of infant hearts
Low-issuing from "The Home." Her children weep
Their more than father, the *one* heart that yearned
With deep paternal interest and pure love
O'er every orphan there! Whose watchful eye
Espied each fault, and sternly, yet in love,
Gave just rebuke—yet ever lent an ear
Of sympathy to all their little woes;
Smiled on their simple joy; and from his tower
Of mental elevation kindly bent,
To share with them in all their pleasant things,
Each of these little ones to his fond heart,
A type of those the gentle Saviour blessed!

O speed ye to the rescue! Lest the flock,
That he led forth to pasture, scatter far,
And hungry wolves devour them in the wild!

And O, ye stricken ones! my brethren dear,
Who worship with me in that humble fane;

Ye, for whose souls he agonized in prayer,
Prostrate all night before the Mercy Seat,
Let not our martyred one have spent in vain
Those bitter sighs and tears, and rendered up
His life in battle, ere the bugle note
Of victory was heard! No—let us up!
And carry on the fight—wage deadly war
Against the bosom sins that caused our Lord
To visit us, so sorely, with distress.

Save, Father!—for without Thee man is vain ;—
Therefore, with bodies prostrate in the dust,
We send our cry beyond the farthest star
Where glow the Seraphim in awful light
Before the Eternal Throne! Blest Spirit! help
With those deep groans which cannot be exprest,
Come to our succor, Lord! Gird on Thy sword,
And, like a mighty giant nerved for war,
Stand forth in our behalf! Not to our cry,
But to the voice of Thy Beloved Son,
Entreating for his spouse—O lend Thine ear,
Nor let Him plead those gory wounds in vain!
February, 1860.

Our Angel Boy.

WHY is it that I cannot sing
    Of thee, our precious Angel boy?
Is it because my heart-strings cling
    Too closely to our buried joy?

When I the solemn chords would sweep,
　And send a requiem o'er thy grave;
I cannot choose but stop and weep,
　So rapidly flows sorrow's wave.

Would I a fragrant wreath entwine
　To place upon thy cherished tomb,
My trembling hands will not combine
　The myrtle and the rose's bloom.

And vividly before my sight
　Sad visions of thy sufferings rise—
Thy spirit striving to take flight;
　Thy mournfully beseeching eyes!

Those lovely orbs of beaming light,
　With pure celestial beauty fraught,
From face to face in rapid flight
　For sympathizing glances sought.

I love and weep—but more than this
　I cannot to my darling give—
But would I from his home of bliss,
　Bear him again on earth to live?

Ah! no—our dovelet safely flew
　Up to the Saviour's tender breast;
No more the ills of life to rue
　Nor ever quit that sheltered nest.

For on our bright redeemèd child,
　God had his signet clearly set,
Grace lay within his bosom mild,
　With dews baptismal duly wet.

Thus when the Angel near his bed
   Stood with his gleaming blade in hand,
His soul knew nor affright, nor dread,
   But smiled upon the glittering brand.

Yes smiles seraphic o'er his face
   In bright succession quickly flew,
As glancing sunbeams when they chase
   The shadows o'er a grassy view!

Within his mother's loving breast
   These treasured tokens safely lie;
She thinks how calm he sank to rest,
   And lifts to Heaven a thankful eye.

She thinks how bright the sun's ray gleamed,
   What time the casement open flew—
What was it to the light that beamed
   That moment on his raptured view!

And is he not her guardian sprite,
   Endowed with cherub virtues now,
To shield her soul in sorrow's night,
   And soothe her spirits when they bow?

And often from her couch she'll rise
   To scan the deep blue arch above,
And fancy that his starry eyes
   Beam on her in undying love.

And I too, as my raptured sight
   Dwells on the sunset clouds of even,
Will fancy that his robes of light
   Gleam through that vista-view of Heaven.

January, 1851.

Flower Strowing.

We went to gather violets
  To strew our darling's bier,
But ere we reached their fragrant homes
  The Snow-King had been there;—
Shaking his plumage as he past,
Borne by the rude boreal blast—
He on the blue-eyed favorites cast
  His icy feathers drear!

Each floweret perished as the barb
  Entered its tender breast;
E'en thus our cherished infant sank
  To his eternal rest;
Lent us a little while to prove
How precious to the heart the love
Of holy Innocence; our Dove
  Soared to its tranquil nest.

With saddened hearts we turned away,
  And eyes suffused with tears,
To seek the odor-breathing plant
  In more congenial spheres.
Kind sympathy the loss supplied
For which our loving bosoms sighed,
Her flowerets had not drooped and died,
  Pierced by the Snow-King's spears.

"Sweets to the Sweet".—thy placid form
  Our darling! on its bier
In simple robe of purest white
  Reposed—a cherub fair!

We strewed it with the purple bloom
Of dewy violets, for the tomb,
Piercing, with eye of Faith, its gloom
  To see thee floating near,

The everlasting fount of Light,
  Dipping thy golden wing
Within its brightly gushing tide,
  Then soaring on to sing
Before the Throne of God the strain
Oft chanted by the ransomed train,
Waiting in blissful hope the reign
  Of Jesus, Glorious King!

"Sweets to the Sweet"—thy grandam dear
  First strewed thy snowy shroud,
With trembling hands and streaming eyes,
  And spirit meekly bowed;
Next she who took thee to her breast,
When her own darling soared to rest
Within the mansions of the Blest
  Above yon radiant cloud!

Thy aunt, thy youthful aunt the third,
  Herself a violet fair—
Watered with sorrow's dew the buds
  She scattered o'er thy bier,
Then in thy hands and on thy breast
I placed my tokens sweet of rest,
And on thy brow a kiss imprest,
  And stroked thy silken hair!

Lo! as we viewed with prayerful glance
  Thy form serene in rest,
The sacred cross is seen inwrought
  Upon thy snowy vest!

Who traced that emblem with the flowers?
Perchance an Angel-hand—or ours
Were guided by mysterious powers
　　To weave that symbol blest!

"Sweets to the Sweet"—thy memory, Love,
　　Soft as the breath of flowers,
Shall float along our devious ways
　　Till Time has told our hours;
Then, as we sink in Death's embrace,
Thy beatific form we'll trace,
Speeding, on wing of light, through space,
　　To welcome to calm bowers!

A Requiem.

HARK! the wintry winds are sighing,
　　Withered leaves our pathway spread;
Strawed by God's own hand in token
　　Of our kindred with the dead:
Yea, the solemn winds are sighing,
　　And the rustling leaves reply,
"Mortal thou art speeding onward—
　　Man thy portion is to die!"

Nor is Nature solely chanting
　　To our hearts this solemn truth;
Hear its dirge-like music floating
　　O'er the faded bowers of youth;
List its mournful echoes rising
　　From our brother's quiet grave,
There he lies in tranquil slumber,
　　Where the hoar oak branches wave.

Early wert thou taken, Brother,
   From our hearts and homes away,
Ere thy rosy youth had brightened
   Into manhood's golden day;
Whilst the flower of Love was blowing
   In thy pure and guileless breast;
Whilst the bird of Hope was building
   'Neath thy eave its peaceful nest.

Shall thy smile no more, my Brother,
   Intellectual, warm and bright—
Greet us with its magic sweetness,
   Cheer us with its witching light?
Never shall thy fond eye-glances
   More by loving friends be seen?
Nor thy proud, majestic forehead,
   Charm us with its grace serene?

Thou wert beautiful, my Brother,
   Beautiful in classic grace,
And the innate virtues glowing
   On thy frank ingenuous face;
Yet a nobler gift was given—
   Gift more precious, more divine,
In thy chaste and pious bosom
   Found the Pearl of Price a shrine!

Pure as water-lily resting
   On the Lake's translucid tide,
On the calm baptismal waters
   Did thy ransomed soul abide;
In thy childhood unpolluted—
   In thy dawning manhood free
From the stormy winds of passion,
   Booming o'er Life's troubled sea!

Wintry winds, lo! ye have borne me
   Where our loved-one mouldering lies;
Leave me not 'mid charnel horrors—
   Waft, O waft me to the skies!
Thither on exulting pinions
   Has our Brother's spirit sped;
Leave me not in grief despondent
   'Mid the cerements of the dead.

He has met his father's spirit;
   Has embraced his cherubs bright;
Has beheld the glorious vision
   Of the Lamb enthroned in Light!
Would we then to earth recall him,
   Bind him to its cares again?
Better far to dwell with Jesus
   In His pure and blissful reign!

What though earth held every blessing
   That could tempt the youthful heart,
He was ready at the summons
   Of the Father to depart;
Leaving to his God his treasures,
   Widowed mother—partner dear—
Child—his dawning star of promise—
   Passed his spirit forth in prayer.

O like him may we be ready
   Ere the awful hour of doom,
When our souls must pass to judgment,
   And our bodies to the tomb;
Then the falling leaves of autumn—
   Then the flowers that faded lie
On our path, no more shall sadden
   When they whisper we must die.

December, 1852.

How Beautiful is Death.

How beautiful is death! how passing fair
Thou restedst Addie,* on thy snowy bier;
    O how serenely calm,
Sweet virgin martyr!—the victorious palm,
    And the triumphal psalm,
Already seem to wave and float around
    Charming our grief profound;
Filling our souls with a mysterious thrill,
Even in that dark hour, to bow us to God's will.

Thy hands were clasped as if in earnest prayer,
As I have often seen them claspéd here:
The pale Japonica upon thy breast
Was not more pure than its still couch of rest;
    Never in Life's wild hour
    Had evil passions power
To enter that abode of Love divine,
    Fair virtue's sacred shrine;
    And as the purple shower,
    Affection's fragrant dower,
Of violets, by hand of Friendship shed
    Within thy coffin bed,
With pleasant odor filled the air and room,
    So, from thy silent tomb,
Thy many virtues shall uprise to calm
The bosom of thy friends, with memory's healing balm.

---

* Adeline Gilmore of Manlius, Western New York, who died at Hyde
Park, St. John's Berkley, January 1st, 1855, from the effects of Yellow
Fever.

O that the mantle of thy soul could rest
    On my perturbéd breast!
Its chaste and holy folds enwrap me quite,
    Calming my wayward spright;
    That even in this hour
    Throbs with wild passion's power,
So that I long to rest my weary head
    Within its clay-cold bed :—
The moonbeams sleep upon thy quiet grave,
The night-winds sigh above the spot, and wave
    The live-oak's mossy arms ;
    To save thee from alarms
Angels encamp around the sacred bowers
    Where, as the seed of flowers,
Each sleeper in his silent cell reposes :
    O! is it sin in me,
    To wish that I could be
Like thee escaped from earthly taint and sorrow,
    Waiting the great To-morrow,
Within the grave where Life's sad drama closes!

Sister of my affection! passed before
    Unto the shadowy shore ;
Nay, passed all shadows—and in glory bright
Walking in snowy robe the fields of light;
    If in thy starry sphere
The disembodied spirit draweth near
    Ever to God in prayer;
Bend thy serene and lily-cinctured brow
    Before the God-head now,
And let thy saintly prayer for me ascend,
Still struggling in this world, my sister and my friend.

Dirge.

Thou hast gone before us
To the silent shore,
Where the stream of sorrow
Welleth never more:
Angel-hands have led thee to repose;
Sweet the crystal river by thee flows.

Like a chiselled image
On an antique tomb
Lies thy sleeping figure
In the vesper gloom;
Chapel-like the little chamber seems,
Lit by solemn moonlight's holy beams.

Angels shall around thee
Through the silent night,
Shed ambrosial dew drops
From their wings of light;
Cherubim with blades of lambent fire,
Demons chase to their abodes of ire.

Scatter purple dew-bells
O'er her snowy bier;
Kiss once more the forehead;
Smoothe the wavy hair.
Dark the lashes of her sealéd eyes,
Shade the cheeks where Death's pale beauty lies!

When the rose-tint flushes
On the brow of morn,

They will tear thee, sister,
From our hearts forlorn;
Stranger hands will place thee in thy grave,
Where the old oak branches sadly wave.

Let us gaze in sorrow
Once more on thee now,
How serenely placid
Beams thy saintly brow!
Clasped thy hands as if in earnest prayer;
Answer spirit! art thou hovering near?

Hark! a voice seraphic
Whispers from the sky,
"Sister, Friends, Companions,
Wipe each tear-dimmed eye,
Lilies gleam not half so pure and fair,
As my blood-washed spirit shineth here."

"Turn your eyes of sorrow
From my clay-cold sod,
In rapt vision follow
To the mount of God;
Angel-friends my spirit now prepare,
Make it meet for yon refulgent sphere."

"I have heard the cherubs
Singing round the Throne;
Caught celestial glimpses
Of the ETERNAL ONE;
Sights seraphical around me rise!—
Paradise is open to mine eyes!"

On the Death of the Rev. J. Ward Simmons.

CLOTHE him in the sacred garment
  By him ever loved the best,
Let the solemn priestly raiment
  His belovèd form invest;
Tenderly let gentle fingers
  Place each snowy fold with care,
As he resteth from his labors
  On his tear-besprinkled bier.

Bury him with solemn music,
  Let the deep-toned organ swell,
And the voices of the choir
  On the hymn and anthem dwell;
Let the words from Heaven uttered,
  Thrill through every nerve and heart—
For he loved his Saviour ever
  To adore with tuneful art.

Tenderly ye Priestly Brothers
  Bear him to his rest profound,
Where the Temple's holy shadow
  Veils the consecrated ground.
Blood-bought! with a mighty spirit
  Thou didst wrestle through the night,
But the Angel hailed thee victor
  With the dawn's returning light!

Happy in the early Autumn,
  With the falling leaves to die,
Ere the chilling blasts of Winter
  Sweep across the darkened sky!

Blessed form! within the quiet
Of the peaceful grave to rest!
Blessed spirit! with the ransomed
Gathered to the Saviour's breast!

See, yon setting sun is shedding
Golden honors o'er him now,
Token of the crown immortal
Soon to sparkle on his brow!
Mourners leave him to his slumber,
Bid your heart-felt sorrow cease;
List! his last triumphant whisper,
"All is peace—Eternal peace."
October, 1854.

Sea-Chimes.

IN MEMORY OF ELIZABETH PORCHER WHITE.

WRITTEN AFTER READING THE OBITUARY IN THE MERCURY OF THE 7TH OF
SEPTEMBER, 1861.

"The innocent child leaves no dark void of sorrow. The sea change
she has undergone spares all other change. She lives on, and can never
grow older. She is forever young in the hearts of her parents."

"SHE has suffered a sea-change,
Into something rich and strange;"
And her innocent young head
Rests upon its rocky bed,
And its Ocean-lavéd pillow,
Lulled by chimings of the billow,

Just as calmly as if Sleep—
Near her mother's heart—did steep
Her fair lids with poppy-dew!—
One can almost fancy too
That her hands are clasped in prayer,
And her coral lips doth wear
A smile, as if a parent's kiss
Her young heart had bathed in bliss.

Ah! say not the sun-beams shock thee—
And the glancing billows mock thee,
As they dance along the strand
Like merry children hand in hand.
On the eye of Sense they rain
Shafts of Light, replete with pain;
To the eye of Faith they beam
Outward symbols of the stream,
Now around thy darling playing
In *the Land* where light is raying
Ever from the Lamb once slain,
Thee and thine to save from pain.

Spirits pure, beneath the billow,
Watch around her shell-wreathed pillow,
Just as surely as they guard,
By the moss-grown church, the yard
Where her kindred sleep in dust
Till the graves give up their trust.

Ah! who knows, but that her rest,
Sweetly on her Uncle's breast—*
Now she taketh—while his arms,
As to shield her from alarms,

---

*Lost in the attempt to save his niece.

Fold her to his loving heart:
Never more from thence to start,
At the booming of the sea,
Till *the angel* sets her free!

This may be a pleasing dream
Caused by moonbeams as they stream
Spirit-like across the sea:—
Stars tell not the mystery—
Though their keen eyes seem to glow
With a light supernal—know,
Eye of Faith alone can read
The mystery of the Holy Creed,
Heart of Faith alone can swell
At the thought that " All is Well "—
That the child is now at rest
On her Saviour's loving breast—
And that brave soul beams a star
Where no billows dash and jar!

On the Death of Mrs. E. C. Gray.

MAY, 1863.

MYSTERIOUS is thine awful presence Death!—
We sat in thoughtful silence in the room
We knew he soon must enter, to bear thence
The immortal from the mortal; to take back
To its Eternal Source the breath of Life
Then quivering in the bosom of *the one*
We watched with loving eyes: Her dearest near,
And a friend loved from childhood's happy morn.

Affection's gaze scarce turned from her calm face;
But soul-intent and riveted by Love
Upon the drooping and dark-fringed lids
Veiling her once bright orbs, thought sure to catch
The last spark thence emitted.   But not so—
Unheard—invisible—on stealthy wing
Death entered and was gone.

    Then came the fresh,
The terrible outburst of anguish, known
Only to those who have endured its sting.—
Here drop the veil, and let the lone heart pour,
In solitude and silence, prayer to God.

What mourn we in thy loss!—A precious gem
Torn from our breast—a chime of sweet bells hushed—
Gloom—where so late was sunshine—and a void
In loving hearts never to be refilled!

True wife—kind friend—and daughter whose soft care
Fell on her widowed mother's sorrowing soul
Like dew-drops on the flowers: Four long years
Her dearest comfort, since *that other* went
To dwell on high with Jesus.   Now *two stars*
The angels number where so late was *one!*

Amid the white-robed band thy Whitsuntide
Thou keepest in the Heavens; where the dew
Of the Eternal Spirit falls more free
Upon thy ransomed and reposing soul,
Enriching and expanding—making meet
For the celestial body yet to spring
From the despoilèd grave—and to its breast
Catch it in perfect union—Deathless—Pure—
E'en as the Lamb's with His pearl-vested Bride!

Little Maggie.

SHE went to dwell beside the sea,
Where ocean's billows, wild and free
　Come bounding to the shore;
The loveliest of the infant band
That gathered shells along the strand,
　And *now* she is no more!

No longer by the sounding sea,
With golden tresses waving free,
　Upon the summer air,
May we her tiny foot-prints trace,
Or watch, with loving eyes, the grace
　Of form and motion rare.

No longer on her mother's breast,
But in the still, deep grave her rest
　She taketh with the host
Of loved and cherished ones, who lie
So calmly 'neath the holy eye
　Of angels at their post—

Keen-watching till the germ of life,
Within the mouldering dust, be rife
　For the immortal bloom—
Then with a beauty, e'en more rare
Than that which veiled her spirit here,
　Exulting from the tomb,

Springs forth her ransomed soul to greet—
Beneath the Great White Throne they meet

Ne'er to be parted more!
And lo! a sweeter voice than e'er
In happy childhood soothed her ear
Floats from the heavenly shore—

"Angel bear up the precious flower,
And place her in her Saviour's bower,
To bloom beneath His eye;
No longer needful of thy care—
But like thee glorious in her sphere;
And nevermore to die!"

The Mountain Rose.

IN MEMORY OF THE YOUNG AND LOVELY MARGARET A. SHOOLBRED.

THE last rosebud has faded
And fallen from the breast,
Where late it lay a thing of life
Caressing and caressed!
Last of the rosy sisters
That blessed a mother's heart,
'Twas sad to see them, one by one,
Droop, wither and depart;
To see them shed their beauty
And drop upon the sod—
Alas! that only Death can lead
To Light—to Life—to God!

How often have we wandered
By lakelet—through the wood—
And I have ever thought thee bright,
And beautiful and good;
5

"The Mountain Rose," I called thee,
   And hoped thy mountain breeze
Would give thee strength and heart and nerve
   To wrestle with disease;
Would with its breath enkindle
   The spark of Life—and set
No fraudful light *upon thy* cheek;
   Nor *in those* eyes of jet.

Alas! for human hoping—
   The light illumined there,
Pure as the star-fires beaming
   From yon celestial sphere,
Shone but to make the darkness
   More dismal when 'twas gone—
Alas! that through the dreary night
   One lone heart must beat on!
Must beat forlorn and shrinking,
   Low murmuring in despair—
Thou, purer than the holy stars!
   O Comforter! draw near.

Whisper in notes far sweeter
   Than voice of plaintive dove,
The great All-Father's chastenings are
   But tokens of His love;
Show how His yearning bosom
   In Earth's dark hour of need,
Sent forth the ONE Begotten
   To suffer and to bleed;
Show to Faith's eye her darlings,
   Made pure by that rich tide,
Clust'ring as fadeless blossoms now
   On bosom of The Bride!

Good Night.

GOOD NIGHT, beloved ones! It is time for me
To launch my bark upon th' unfathomed sea
That laves the headland of Eternity,
Good night!

My skiff heaves with the billow—and the air
Seems full of strange, sad whispers. Do I hear
The spirit voices of the unknown sphere?
Good night!

Methinks a storm is brooding in the sky—
The stars have bid good night—the moon is shy
To show her face in Heaven—come, draw ye nigh,
Good night!

Draw nigh—nor while I linger let me miss
The warm, soft pressure of each loving kiss—
They take me back to days of childish bliss,
Good night!

To days when by my Mother's knee I prayed;
Or with ye, sisters, on the white sand strayed—
This is another sea—I'm half afraid—
Good night!

Good night! Good night! O it is hard to go—
But all those airy voices call me so—
I must depart—Beloved! *That voice* I know,
Good night.

It is my Mother's! and it chides delay,
And bids me trust in ONE has led the way
Over Death's gloomy tide—I fain obey,
                              Good night.

Good night!   The gloom is almost gone—a ray
Strikes on yon headland from approaching day—
Sweet sisters one last kiss—and now away
                              To Light!

The Double Harvest.

'TIS the glorious time of harvest—
    And the sun is shining clear,
Shooting rays of golden beauty
    Through the azure fields of air;
Downward darts the heavenly radiance
    Till the reapers sickles gleam
Like a fiery flash of glory
    In the bright, refulgent beam!

Lo! on bronzed and stalwart shoulders,
    Homeward now the sheaves are borne,
And the harvest chant is ringing
    Upward to the Father's throne!
Hark! is that its joyous echo
    Striking sweetly on our ear?
God! it is the cry of anguish,
    Bitter anguish and despair!

For the reaper Death is busy,
    And a double harvest-home
Through the land is being gathered,—
    Death has entered many a dome;

Cutting down with scythe resistlesss
  The beloved on every side—
Feeble eld—and youth of promise ;
  Cherished babe—and blooming bride.

" Rachel weepeth for her children "—
  And *thy* heart my friend is torn,
Death has been among thy flowers,
  And thy brightest bud has borne
To his cold and silent bower
  Where it very safely lies
Hidden—but not lost forever—
  From thy fond maternal eyes!

Thou hast given up thy darling
  To his Saviour and his God,
And thy bleeding heart submissive
  Bows beneath His chastening rod ;
And the holy faith within thee
  Comes to comfort and to calm ;
And the Spirit on thy bosom
  Sheds his pure and healing balm.

Ah ! sad father, bowed with anguish,
  Lift from darksome earth thine eye ;
Thy beloved one has been garnered
  To a peaceful home on high !
There his youth shall know no tarnish,
  There his virtues shall expand,
Till the Resurrection morning
  Find him 'mid the chosen band.

Find him, with the ransomed thousands,
  Near the Saviour's Throne of Light,

Intellectual beauty beaming
    In his eye divinely bright!
Then those proud hopes fondly cherished,
    Now crushed-out, bereaved ones! here,
Shall revive to glow forever
    In that sinless, deathless sphere.

There may the once perfect circle—
    Now unlinked—in rapture meet,
Ne'er again to be dissevered,
    But in harmony complete
Move along those countless ages,
    Drawing nearer all the while;
To the Throne of God Eternal—
    To the brightness of His smile.
September, 1858.

Helen.

DEDICATED TO DR. B. A. RODRIGUES, OF CHARLESTON, S. C.,

ON THE DEATH OF HIS DAUGHTER.

I WELL remember thy sweet flower,
Thy Helen! with her glorious dower
Of graces that enriched thy bower;

Making it innocently bright;
A moonlit glade of softened light
From sun of the primeval Height.

She was a little airy thing,
When first she did around me fling
The witchery of which I sing.

It holds me still in fairy wise,
The beauty of those dove-like eyes,
That took me then by sweet surprise.

So gleesome, yet so free of guile—
So full of childish grace—her smile
So calculated to beguile

The heart of woe—and mine was sad;
'Twixt swell of hope and fear half mad—
She came between and made me glad.

'Twas on a sultry summer's day,
The river sparkled in its ray—
The steamer sped upon her way.

But thou and thine were blithe and gay
On that *remembered* summer day;
Now Death has crossed *thy* gladsome way.

I ever loved thy precious flower,
The pride, the darling of thy bower,
And followed her through girlhood's hour

With glance of tenderness—and knew
That as to womanhood she grew
Her beauty took a richer hue;

Until thy "Wildbrier" did assume
The Rose's majesty and bloom,
Her beauty and *her rich perfume.*

But when she left the parent bower,
Another holier home to dower,
With all her wealth of love—that hour

I lost her from my sight—yet *there*
I never doubted but as clear
A light she shed as otherwhere.

Making the wedded homestead bright
As if an angel shed the light
So soon to be exchanged for night.

Too soon her wingéd sisters bore
Her spirit to the eternal shore,
Where peace abideth evermore.

And if she little ones have left
To fill the chasm Death has cleft
In the sad hearts of her bereft;

O! may *another Helen* spring
From *them,* around thy neck to cling!
On thy declining life to fling

The beauty and the joy that erst
Beamed on thy pathway from *the first,*
The child thy loving heart had nurst,

Hoping her gentle hand should close
Thine eyelids for their last repose;
But the Almighty Father knows

Best—and He took thy spotless flower
To bloom within His Heavenly Bower:—
Bow in submission to the Power

That chastens us in love—and feel
The freeness of His grace to heal
When in undoubting faith we kneel

And render of our very best:
Such anguish wrung the Patriarch's breast
Upon Moriah's cloudy crest.

Oh! may the Patriarch's God, and thine
Lead *thee* along the Way Divine,
Until thou reach the Inner Shrine
Where Helen beameth now, beneath the Eye benign!
Summerville, March 1st, 1866.

Christ : The Rock.

DEVOTED TO THE MEMORY OF A BELOVED FRIEND AND COUSIN.

THE simple record of her end, what peace it sheds
    around!—
Unbind the sandals from your feet, for this is holy ground.
Tread softly—let no jarring sound nor echo meet her
    ear;
Breathe softly—utter not a word—the dying is in prayer!

"Be quiet, only let me feel that ye are very near,
Press the warm kiss upon my brow, toy with my wavy
    hair;
Pet me, as ye were wont to do—ye know I love it so,
Friends! let me feel that ye are here when I am called
    to go.

Thoughts of 'The Valley' used to fill my heart with
    gloom and fear,
But lo! the valley is all bright—I see my Saviour there,

Light'ning it with His victor crown ; His smile serenely
    calm,
Sheds for the festering wounds within a softly soothing
    balm."

'Tis noon—high noon—the hour when He sat weary on
    the well,
And she is weary, and would leave this world with Him
    to dwell ;
And Christ has come—she feels Him near—The Rock
    whose friendly shade
Maketh the fiery furnace seem a cool, refreshing glade.

Yes, he has come to take her where her mother waits
    to fold
Her daughter in her loving arms, with raptures mani-
    fold ;
And every shade, and every tear has dimmed *that*
    daughter's face
Shall roll, as cloud-drifts from the sun, beneath that
    warm embrace.

Breathe low ! there is a whisper near, a murmur in the
    pines,
Far off a partridge drops her note—the sweet, soft, sum-
    mer winds
Just wave the curtains to and fro—is there another
    sound ?
The rustle of an angel's wing?—Her soul has passed
    the bound !

It wings its flight above the clear, expanding, azure sky ;
O ! she will never more have cause to breathe the low,
    sad sigh,

That pine-trees bar the glorious view of God's o'er-arch-
    ing Heaven,
Now to her pure and cleanséd sight such brighter scenes
    are given!

Now that she dwells with the redeemed in those deli-
    cious bowers,
Where God pours down a richer beam than that'en-
    lightens ours;
Where all the air is musical with Dove-notes soft and
    clear;
Where Jesus breathes the breath of peace on saints
    reposing there!
    Summerville, July 11th, 1866.

The Martyr Boy.

DEDICATED TO THE MEMORY OF HENRY L. DUNHAM, WHO
DIED AT ABINGTON, MASS., MAY 25, 1867, AGED 18
YEARS, 8 MONTHS AND 17 DAYS.

    " They shall walk with me in white; for they are worthy."

    SHE weeps!—my sister weeps!—
Weeps for her first-born; for her martyr boy;
At once her greatest trial, purest joy;—
For eighteen years he bore his heavy cross;
For *him* to die is gain—to *her* the loss;
Only a mother's heart can understand
With what a strong, mysterious, holy band
God knit his life to her's. A mother's love!
Not angels dwelling near its fount above
Can penetrate its depth! But One alone,

The Prince of Love, now seated on His throne,
Can understand its length and depth and height—
He holds *this* key of knowledge by His right
As son of God and man; His infant rest
Was on a Virgin's pure, maternal breast!

     With what a thrill of joy
My sister pressed her first—her darling boy
To her soft throbbing heart! No lovelier flower
Ere spread its petals in a nuptial bower
Than this sweet bud—large starry eyes of blue,
Taking their tint from the autumnal hue
Of the o'er-arching sky;—plump, rosy, bright,
A child of beauty—filling with delight
All hearts susceptive of the heavenly wile
That plays around an infant's artless smile;
Who could have dreamed that anything amiss
Would mar the rapture of the welcome kiss
Pressed on his sweet, soft mouth! That his smooth brow
Would wrinkle o'er with pain; his bosom, now
So pure and yielding, should be made to bear
The pelting of Life's storm for many a sad, long year!

Soon as her boy began to go alone
The mother's heart assumed an anxious tone;
All was not right; as year on year sped by
Her fear increases; and her loving eye
Follows him ever with uneasy glance,
Lest to his infant limbs some sad mischance
Should happen; for tho' rosy, well and gay,
He cannot move about, and run, and play
As other boys—he tottered in his gait,
As if his body were too great a weight

For his frail limbs and tiny feet to bear ;
Oh then in secret many an earnest prayer
Sped to the ONE who dries the mourner's tear !   .

Physicians were consulted—none gave hope;
Some thought that when his wondering eyes did ope
Upon this world of beauty, at his side
Stood this affliction, as a spectre bride,
To darken all his life; some deemed a fall,
Or other accident unknown, this pall
Of blackness had about his cradle cast
Beneath whose cruel shade his youthful days were past.

Our greatest Surgeon spoke his candid mind—
" No art of man a remedy can find
For this poor boy; and ere he pass away   .
The light of reason from his mind shall stray
Leaving it dark and void."—Thank God in *this*
The learned Physician thought and spoke amiss !
Clear, bright and beautiful did ere remain
His spirit, tho' his limbs were racked with pain ;
Tho' on his couch from year to year he lay
Helpless, around his active brain would play
Thoughts rich and wonderful—he converse held
With the sublimest souls ; from books he drew
Their treasured wisdom; with Pierian dew
Stored the deep cells of his retentive mind ;
An answer to each question could he find
At any moment ; from his bosom welled,
As from a crystal fount, the Holy Truth
Learnt from a mother's love and sympathizing ruth !

And she who made him from the first her care,
By Providence was led to spend a year—

The last sad year of his short life—with him!
The nine long ones of absence seemed a dream
When seated by his side. She heard him read;
Built up his faith in the most holy creed
Learnt in his Southern home; when for the dove,
But two months lent to stir the fount of love
In all their breasts, from pious lip and heart,
Over its "casket" ere 'twas laid apart,
Went up the words of prayer—she by his plane
Sat, wiping tears, that fell like summer rain,
From his sad eyes—and little thought the day
Was speeding on when God would wipe away
        His last sad tear,
        And in a painless sphere,
Open those loving eyes which beamed so brightly here!

          Weep, weep no more!
Your child has gained the safe, refulgent shore!
      He who on earth could stir nor hand, nor feet,
      Now with angelic pinions fleet
      Cleaves the pure ether—'round the height
      Of the celestial Eden wings his flight!
      No longer on his plane
      Must night and day remain;
      But on a bed of roses
      His long tried, patient soul reposes—
      Guarded by cherubs bright;
      And smiling on his sight,
The spirit of his infant brother weaves
A garland for his brow of never dying leaves!

And lo! the Man of Grief, who bore His cross
So meekly up the rugged mountain side,
Bends over him, and bids his ransomed Bride

To wrap him in the mantle of her love,
And cause the soothing music of the Dove
    Float by to charm his rest
    Within his rosy nest;
    Where cleansed from earthly dross,
    No more he suffers loss—
But with the Saints in calm delight awaits
The bursting of the bars that bind the pearly gates!

The Shepherd's Call.

"He calleth his own sheep by name."
"I am the Good Shepherd, and know my sheep, and am known
of mine."

It was not strange, my little dear,
    That God should call our Henry hence;
    He goes to meet his recompense,
His crown of martyrdom to wear.

The Shepherd knoweth all His sheep,
    And calleth each to Him by name,
    And they were very much to blame
If they should earthward turn and weep.

He calleth for a little lamb—
    It leaps and bounds into his arms;
    He folds it safe from all alarms:
No more it bleateth for its dam.

He calleth one of larger growth—
    He finds Earth's sunny pastures fair;
    Her flowerets lovely—balm her air;
And turneth from them somewhat loth.

The Shepherd meets and leads him where
 He sees the heavenly meadows green,
 By angel-hands kept fresh and clean;
The winding river cool and clear!

He calleth to His sheep—they come
 From where they lie, at heat of day,
 Toil-worn and weary of the way,
And follow very gladly home!

He calls the aged of the flock—
 They have sucked poison from Earth's flowers;
 Found serpents in her fairest bowers;
And wounded feet upon the rock.

Therefore most gladly do they hear
 His silvery accents calling "home"—
 And answer "blessed Lord we come"
To breathe the Balm of Eden air.

And may our little one be given
 The grace all-lovingly to go,
 When the Good Shepherd whispers low,
"Come taste the pasturage of Heaven!"

My Unknown Friend.

I HAVE a friend—an unknown friend,
 Far o'er the billowy sea;
And O! I wish he would transmit
 A letter unto me!
I sent him one I deemed would reach
 His home by Christmas Day,
Or if not on that happy tide,
 With New Year's dawning ray.

I have a friend—a learnéd friend,
  Old England's gifted son!
To whom her martyrs from their graves
  In chorus cry "well done,"
"Well done"—for thou hast nobly stood
  In trial's fearful hour,
And battled for old England's church—
  Her sure abiding tower!

Old England's Church—the Church of Christ,
  Has ever been his theme,
In her good cause he sacrificed
  Each rainbow-tinted dream—
Each rainbow dream—each starry hope,
  Bright visions fair of youth,
He sacrificed them all to aid
  The sacred cause of truth!

I have a friend—a poet friend,
  One of the choral band
Who send the music of their harps
  O'er Albion's happy land ;
Nor only on her sea-girt shores
  Their Heaven-strung harps rebound,
Their echoes reach our western wilds
  And 'wake responsive sound!

And when like David they have vowed
  Their deep-toned Lyres to Heaven,
Then, what a magical effect
  To each rich chord is given!
A power to move the sternest breast—
  To make the gentle weep—
To soothe the heaving bosom, when
  Dark sorrows o'er it sweep!
  6

Thus Keble is a name to love;
    Milman a spell to bind;
Heber a beacon when our bark
    A peaceful port would find;
Williams—but O! I cannot tell
    What *he* has been to me,
Williams! my kind, my unknown friend,
    Far o'er the billowy sea!

With him I've wandered in the gloom
    Of old "CATHEDRAL" aisle,
And trembled while the organ filled
    With solemn swell the pile;
Or listened while in cadence sweet
    He of the martyrs told,
Now resting in their antique tombs—
    Or carved in marble cold.

With him I've stood and gazed upon
    The pure "BAPTISTERY'S" flood,
Until methought the crystal wave
    Was tinged with Jesus' blood;
So awfully each sentence fell
    How His sad death obtains
To make this, seeming, simple flood
    Wash out the vilest stains!

With him I've mused on by-gone scenes,
    Till "THOUGHTS OF PAST YEARS" came
Too vividly before my sight
    And roused cold memory's flame;
With him I've trod the narrow "WAY"
    That leads to "LIFE ETERNE,"
Enlightened by the rays that gleam
    Whence Love's pure altars burn.

With him I've read and *sung* by turns
    The "PASSION OF OUR LORD,"
Until mine inmost spirit longed
    For his life-giving word;
And if my bosom hath received
    The Spirit warm and free,
I owe, through God, in part the thanks
    Dear, unknown friend,—to thee!
January, 1851.

The Children of the Church Home.

I LOVE these children Lord,
    These little lambs of Thine;
The flock redeeming love has called
    To pasture near Thy shrine.

O keep them safely there—
    Protect them from all harms,
O tender Shepherd! kindly bear
    These nurslings in Thine arms.

How sweet on Sabbath-day,
    Within thine House of Prayer,
To list their infant voices rise
    To Heaven in accents clear.

To hear them swell the hymn;
    To hear them lisp the creed,
Whose holy doctrines sage of old
    Had vainly sought to read.

To see them meekly kneel ;
  The penitential sigh
To waft with contrite sinners up,
  In faith, beyond the sky.

These wayside flowers of earth,
  By Jesus' loving care,
Were brought to bloom within the gate
  Of God's own Eden fair.

Oh! who with ruthless hand
  Would cast them forth again,
To wither 'neath the summer's sun
  Or Winter's chilly rain!

O rather may each soul,
  Redeemed by Heavenly power,
Pray that the dews of Grace may fall
  Upon each bud and flower.

Rather may Christian hands,
  With gentle fostering care
These tender plants about the Tree
  Of Life assist to rear!

For angels on *That Day*
  When Christ shall claim His own,
From them a garland shall entwine
  Around His glorious Throne!

1858.

Little Bet.

A LITTLE fairy creature draped in white—
She bounded in the room and sprang within
The arms of our loved Pastor: A pure dove
She seemed snug-nestled there in perfect trust
And calm confiding love; or feeble lamb
Borne by the tender Shepherd on his breast.
Sweet Innocence upon Religion stayed—
Fair type of the affection deep we owe
The blesséd Jesus; and th' undoubting faith
We should repose in Heaven. Make us LORD,
Like this, Thine infant daughter, pure and true !

Little Harriet.

SHE is a winsome, precious pet,
    A darling blue-eyed dove ;
The sweetest little nursling yet
Has caught me in the golden net
    Of its pure, baby love !

She came in sorrow's blackest night
    Its darkness to illume ;
A beam of the celestial light—
A little comfort-freighted sprite,
    She flitted in the gloom.

But soon upon her pearly vest,
   We spied the taint of sin;
The precious dovelet of our nest—
Our darling, Heaven-commissioned guest,
   Bore the death-spot within!

So at the Holy Whitsuntide
   We took her to the stream,
That ever from the Saviour's side
Flows forth to cleanse His mystic bride
   And make her brightly beam!

From thence our baby bore a dower
   Of beauty, far more rare
Than that which decks the Lily-flower,
Or blushes in the Rose's bower
   When Spring is breathing near!

And I have vowed this child to be
   An almoner of Heaven;
Her dimpled hands shall scatter free—
Into the Saviour's treasury,
   Her gifts shall all be given.

And may the Triune God indeed
   Confirm my heart-deep prayer,
Safely her tiny footsteps speed
In the old pathways to the meed
   Of the Eternal Sphere!

May her whole life a mission prove
   To loved ones young and old;
The moist rays of soul-pitying love
Beam from the soft eyes of our dove
   To win into The Fold,

Sad, erring spirits, wandering far
  In regions drear and lone,
Until the pearly gates unbar,
And show our babe a burning star
  Before the Saviour's throne.

March 13, 1860.

Confirmation

AT ST. JOHN'S CHAPEL, HAMPSTEAD, MARCH 25, 1860.

It is the vesper tide
  And Evening, like a bride,
Sits blushing in her gorgeous western bower;
  Waiting the regal Night,
  To veil her glowing light
And lead her to his star-emblazoned tower!

But not the bridal sweet
  When Eve and Night shall meet,
Hath charmed us forth at close of Sabbath-day;
  Leave to the poet's eye
  The glories of the sky,
When Nature weaves their nuptial garlands gay.

Espousals holier thrill
  Our Christian hearts—and fill
Our human eyes with happy, rapturous dew;
  A soul flings off its clod
  And springs to meet its God,
As tender plants burst forth to cheer the view.

O make it truly thine,
Father and Friend divine!
And set thy seal confirmal to the vow,
That erst in faith was made,
When *she*, now sainted, laid
Her precious one before Thy throne—but now

She is not here to see
Her first-born bend the knee,
And bow his youthful head with reverence meet;
To list the voice of prayer
Float on the buoyant air
In undulating waves of music sweet.

From her bright resting star
An angel points afar
To the green earth that once she called her home;
Following his golden trace
Along the fields of space
She marks this humble, consecrated dome—

Where, calm and most serene
The holy man is seen
Clothed with authority from God on High,
To bless with Jesus' love
Each trembling, timid dove
That to the riven Rock would gladly fly.

As on the happy day
She watched his first essay
To poise his little frame and walk alone;
So now her beaming eye,
Love-lighted, from the sky
Sees this first step towards the Heavenly Zone.

Lo! with maternal care
She spreads her arms, for fear
Her tender one should stumble by the way;
She cannot reach him here—
And now her eyes in prayer
Are lifted to the realms of endless day,

" Father! my first-born joy
Save from Earth's sad annoy,
And lead in safety through the howling Wild—
Blest Spirit grace impart;
Jesus with loving art
Woo to Thy breast my precious, darling child."

Confirmation.

LOVED one! whose body moulders in yon grave
Marked by the sacred emblem of the cross,
But whose immortal spirit long has passed
Into the rest which is not indolence;
But that sublime repose and heavenly calm
Laid up in store for all the dead in Christ!
O from that sphere—wherever it revolves,
In the illimitable Space of God,
On its harmonious axis 'round the Throne
Of the All-Loving Heart—hast thou beheld
The scenes enacted here? Scenes that had stirred
Thy pure, maternal heart if still on Earth,
To its serenest depth! I cannot think
That the beloved departed ever nigh—

7

Close as the atmosphere that wraps us 'round—
Know every thought and throb of our proud hearts
Still struggling in this gloom; if they maintain
Affections, kin to those that moved them here,
They would too keenly suffer when we sinned.
Yet verily subscribe this cheering creed—
That when such scenes occur in this our Orb,
May add new rapture to the souls in Bliss,
Jehovah sends some bright, angelic power
To point the same to their adoring gaze;
Then the commissioned Seraph lifts the veil
That hides our green-robed earth; and makes the ken
Of the reposing spirit strike its disk
And draw new draughts of light and love from thence.
Thus, dear one, I believe that thou hast seen
The wonders God has wrought in thy beloved,
Thy first-born, the beginning of the joy
Maternal—which welled up so pure and fresh
For all the sons that followed.   The dear lamb
Thou broughtest rejoicing to the Saviour's fold,
And laid, in faith, upon His tender breast,
To be renewed by water and His Grace!—
And now, by virtue of that Love Divine,
Has he progressed and taken his first step
In Christian Life.   But two short weeks agone
He bowed his youthful head in meekness low,
And "trembling at the sacred rail" received
The imposition of anointed hands,
With benediction wedded to deep prayer.
Well I remember when he first essayed
To take his primal step, on Earth—alone,
How tenderly thou watched him—what delight
Beamed in thy dark, deep eyes; raying, star-like,

From shadow of the long, black, silken fringe.
How thy fond arms extended, circling 'round
To shield thy child from harm! E'en thus, methought,
I saw thee stretch them forth when his first step
He took alone upon the heavenly road,
As thou wouldst guard him from more serious fall.
And lo! a whisper, softer than the voice
Of turtle cooing 'mid the tender vines,
Comes floating to thine ear: "Not thy weak arms,
But the Almighty Saviour's must enfold
And bear thy child uninjured through the Wild."
" Trust all to God in Him!" And then thine eyes
Turned in their dewy trustfulness to Heaven,
Where that great Human Heart beats warm and true,
On the Eternal Throne at God's right hand,
Yet still is touched by feeling of our need,
Having when on Earth been tempted like to us,
Yet keeping free from every taint of Sin.

First Communion.

EASTER-SUNDAY—APRIL 8TH, 1860.

No mortal has done this! The hand of God
Alone has set the seed. The dew of Grace
Fell from His urn in soft, refreshing showers,
More potent than the first and latter rain,
Causing this tender shoot to grow and thrive,
A young plant in the Temple of His Son!
Therefore with hearts rejoicing go we up
To keep the Feast of Feasts! The risen Christ,

Meets in the garden with a solemn "Hail"
This youthful heart, and bids it come with Him
And rest awhile upon the Lily beds,
Within His spicy bowers—There, in peace,
To list the whisper of the Spirit Dove.

O happy thus in youth to taste of Heaven!
Before the clutch of Sin has held thee tight,
And thy release cause wrestling and keen pain!
Now rather all is joy!   And Earth and Heaven
Seem brought in contact by a golden stair,
On which bright angels travel to and fro,
And by whose rounds thou too mayest mount to God!

Blest Easter! by thy Mother loved so well—
Which ever through her bosom sent a thrill
Of pure and holy joy!   'Twas meet that thou,
Her son, should consecrate this sacred time
By giving up thyself entire to God
In body, soul and spirit.   Drawing near,
In full assurance, and most earnest faith,
Unto the Holy Table of thy Lord,   .
There to receive the mystic bread and wine,
Shall make thee reach the perfect man in Christ.

For this our prayer ascendeth.   And when thou,
In Adam shall have paid the debt of Life,
God grant, in Christ, thou mayest be made alive,
And in His heavenly Kingdom share the bliss
Of those departed in His faith and fear!

Thoughts During Convention.

MAY, 1860.

Two absent from the assembly of The Church—
From our small portion of the Fold Divine,
The vast Christ-purchased Body Catholic!
'Gainst which the gates of Hell shall not prevail;
Whose glorious chart is written in His blood,
And sealed with the Eternal seal of God,
Impressed by His right hand of love and power.
Two absent—and our tears attest the deep
And fond emotion of our troubled souls,
As our sad eyes vainly seek out their forms.
One nevermore shall sit in council here!—*
His place henceforth is with the sainted dead,
The sacramental hosts of God's elect,—
To rest with Christ until th' Eternal Dawn.

The other—and our hearts go with him—bears
His heavy cross along Life's dreary way,
On trial in the furnace of sharp pain.
Our venerable Father! †   How we miss
His calm presiding presence—the repose,
Almost sublime, of his pure, classic brow;
The deep serene of the angelic face
From whence all trace of sin has been expelled:

---

* Rev. Cranmore Wallace.
† Bishop Davis—at this time in the hand of a skilful Northern oculist.

Those sweet, sad eyes, earth-veiled, yet filled with
    light—
The Light which lighteth every soul redeemed.
And oh Thou Light! who, when upon our Orb,
Not only shed'st Thy ray within the soul,
Chasing the darkness from that deep recess,—
But whose true human and most loving heart,
Pitying our sad infirmities, sent health,
And strength and vigor through our sin-racked frames;
Who healed'st the sick—restored'st the dead to life;
And drov'st the Demons from dark, troubled souls—
Be with us in this hour of sore distress,
And from thy Kingly Throne in highest Heaven,
Hear our sad cry for our beloved head—
Our dear afflicted Bishop! With Thine hand
Break the firm seals that hold the precious sight
Deep in its secret cell. The visual nerve,
Rewakened by thy touch, shall drink in light,
Beauty and joy,—from earth, and sea, and sky!

But if—within the depths of Love Divine—
The predetermined counsel of God's will
Has ordered otherwise. *That will be done:*
Make *us* to bow submissive; and *his* soul
Fill with such floods of the celestial ray
As shall expel all darkness, and make clear
All that seems now inscrutable. As gloom
Deepens and deepens outward—greater light
Pour in, until the introverted glance,
Purged from the sights of earth, with holy John
Views that bright Home, whose light is from the Lamb!

Easter Eve.

A FRAGMENT.

'Tis a sweet, quiet eve—The sun has sunk
Behind the forest trees, yet still the heavens
Reflect his dazzling ray and richly glow
With crimson, gold and sapphire. To the east
A peaceful lakelet lies, beneath the smile
Of the full Paschal moon, around whose edge
The weeping willows droop their graceful heads,
And with their feathery branches stir the wave
Dimpling its face with beauty. 'Tis an hour
Of deep, mysterious calmness—All the world
Seems resting in tranquillity and peace
As if it held a Sabbath, or reposed
With Jesus in the quiet sleep of death
Waiting the great uprising. Not a sound
Disturbs the awful stillness of the scene,
Save when a passing zephyr stirs the trees
Making their graceful branches kiss the tide.
Not e'en the mock-bird's merry note is heard,
Nor wailing of the lonely whippoorwill.
Now o'er the beaming visage of yon orb,
Night's radiant queen, the pure, refulgent moon,
A floating cloud has flung a silvery veil;
And now a thick, black pall has hid her face,
But lo! she breaks through the obscuring mist,
And casts the veil of darkness from her brow!
Thus may my soul burst through each darksome shroud
And float serenely on the track of Heaven.

Whit-Sunday.

SUMMERVILLE, 1866.

DEDICATED TO THE REV. J. A. HARROLD, PASTOR OF THE CHURCH.

MORNING.

It was the Festival of Whitsuntide—
The Church assembled waited as of yore
The coming of the blessed Paraclete,
The Lord and source of Life, whose advent He,
The once abased, but now exalted Son,
Had promised from The Father; who proceeds
Alike from both—with both as God adored!

Within the chancel stands the aged priest,*
So long the well-loved pastor of this Flock;
Resigned with pain, yet with submissive faith
And confidence in the unerring love
Of the great Shepherd who from his weak grasp,
Weakened by sickness and declining life,
Had gently ta'en the pastoral staff—and placed
The sacred trust in younger, stronger hands.
Meekly he stands, in snowy vesture clad,
Beside the Altar waiting to assist
The Rector at the Eucharistic feast,
Who meanwhile with clear, earnest voice intoned
Our solemn ritual.   Pale he is, and weak
From recent illness, but he needs must come

---

* The Rev. Philip Gadsden, for thirty-seven years Rector of St.
Paul's Church, Summerville.

To feed his Master's Flock within the wild,
By love and duty prompted. Now he reads
From the blessed Word of God, how wicked men
In early ages served the Infant Church,
And how *she* grew beneath the fiery scourge.
But lo! he stops, he trembles, he bows down—
He lays his head in his extended palm—
Reels—would have fallen, had not anxious friends
Flown to his aid—and borne his fainting form
Into the Vestry-room, amid the tears,
And startled gaze of his awe-stricken flock!

Say, is it life or death? Life! Life! He lifts,
Slowly, the drooping purple-tinted lids
From his dark eyes and life is beaming there,
Tho' dimly in a little feeble spark!

The aged minister with faint, low voice,
Made fainter by deep feeling, now takes up,
From where 'twas broken off, the sacred Form,
And finishes the Daily Morning Prayer.
The sermon is omitted—yet or ere
He goes towards the Altar thence to take,
Within his priestly hands the bread and wine,
And after Consecration give them round,
No longer common food, to those who kneel
In lively faith and penitential love—
The door is gently opened, and in glides,
More like a pallid ghost than living man,
The Rector, and once more resumes his place
To minister the Sacramental Rite
Of Holy Baptism—to one who waits,
All sadly clad in sorrow's gloomy weeds,
To be received and made the Child of God.

EVENING.

A flutter of white garments and the tramp
Of infant feet along the pleasant path
Leading unto the little village church;
See, through the windows, how they flit along
The little innocent things! all wreathed in smiles,
And bearing fragrant flowers in their hands,
Meet offering of fresh childhood unto God!—

'Tis evening—and the second lesson o'er
They enter, singing blithely as the birds,
Their Father's House;—as those blessed ones of old
On whom the gracious Saviour showered praise
And move towards the Altar—where *he* stands,
Their Pastor!—from his bed of suffering come.—
Waiting with loving heart, his gentle lambs,
Oh! 'twas a sight the angels must have loved
To look upon! The pastor's kindly eye
Filled with soft tears—and not an eye or heart
Within the church but sympathized with his.
They passed up by the aisle, those boys and girls
Bearing their blossoms—and on either hand
Parting, arrange themselves in order meet
On both sides of the chancel, and adown
The middle aisle—still singing their glad song,
And see, two little ones—all fairy-like,
And lovely as the angels;—One with wild,
Dark, eager eyes 'neath brow replete with thought,
And features o'er whose winsome innocence
The light of genius flashes, and lights up
The whole with beam of Heaven! The other pet,
A slender child, with soft, blue, loving eyes;
And golden ringlets rippling o'er her neck—

Bearing a tiny basket decked with flowers,
Within which, closely sealed, the offering lay,
Collected from these little ones to aid
The cause of Missions in the Heathen Land.
At signal from the pastor they approach,
And kneeling at the chancel, place within
His ready hand the offering of the school,
Then flit away, like timid doves, and take
Their place among the children of The Fold.

The pastor in few, simple words explains,
And speaks to them of Holy Whitsuntide—
How Catechumens in the Early Times,
All robed in snowy white, were on this day
Admitted, by baptism, to the Church—
They, too, had all been members made of Christ;
Children of God, and heirs of Life Divine;
And wore white robes in token of the same.
See to it, that ye keep your hearts unsoiled
By stain of sin—as Christian children should;
Then shall the angels bear ye when ye die
To live with Christ forever in the skies!—

Once more their youthful voices join in song:
The Benediction followed—and the love
Of God the spirit nestled in each heart.

Sonnet.

TO MY NEPHEW—H. L. D.

How much of suffering has been thine, Dear boy,
  In this terrestrial sphere! Thy span of years,
  Rounded a dozen amid sighs and tears,
And dark o'er hanging clouds. Yet bright-eyed joy
Peeped, ever and anon, with glances coy,
  From out the murky veil, and flashed the light
  Of Hope celestial o'er thy saddened spright,
And leaving thee sweet flowers with which to toy!

All lone and cheerless hitherto thy lot—
  Save when, for Jesus' sake, some Christian heart
Took pity on the exile—and thy cot
  Blessed with his holy tendance. Now thou art
Surrounded by thy dear ones, and may rest
Thy aching head upon thy Mother's breast!
  January, 1861.

Old Jack.

Thou hoary patriarch of ninety-seven,
Waiting thy summons to the Court of Heaven;
How do I grieve to leave thee here alone,
Without one mind congenial to thine own;
Without a friend to ope the sacred scroll,
And pour the light celestial on thy soul -

Streaming from every line ; to lead thy thought
Far from the world's turmoil to Him who wrought
For thy redemption, and His life-blood shed
A gory tide, on Calvary's rugged head !

Ah, yes !—I grieve to leave thee groping here
In twofold darkness—desolate and drear—
Thy visual orb closed to the golden day ;
In vain the brilliant flowers along thy way ;
In vain will pleasant corn-fields wave and veer
Their bright green foliage in the Summer air,
And sable rustics bind th' Autumnal grain,
And bear the golden sheaves for thee in vain !

But sadder yet to think the sacred page
To thee is sealed as for a little age ;
The long, long Summer-tide must come and go,
Ere thou shalt list its holy precepts flow
From lip of mistress dear—or Pastor friend ;
Or, one unworthy who yet loves to blend
Her voice with thine in solemn prayer or hymn,
While holy feeling mounting to the brim
Runs o'er her soul—and floats within her eyes
In supplication glancing to the skies.

And I have seen thee weep right bitter tears,
O'er sins and follies of thy early years ;—
O may they all be treasured up on high,
Where God himself shall wipe from every eye
Contrition's dew—and turn to gems of light
To deck the Saviour's Coronal—more bright
Than those of Seraphim, who wheel their cars
Above the golden orbit of the stars,
Or sainted elders' chaplets, only meet
To form a pavement for Jehovah's feet !

Nor thou alone—but all the aged band,
Approaching surely to the shadowy strand,
I leave regretful! O Almighty King!
Keep them securely 'neath thy sheltering wing;
In life or death be Thou their constant stay,
Thine Angel lead them on their darksome way,
Should Summer-shaft their feeble bodies wound;
Or blasts Autumnal lay them on the ground
Like withered leaflets—may their end be peace—
Their spirits garner in that isle where cease
All sin and sorrow, to await the dawn
Shall part the curtain of ærial lawn,
And pour upon their long expected eyes
The dazzling glory of the UPPER SKIES!

May, 1857.

The Sad Heart.

HEART! wherefore art thou sad?
Does not the Sun glance lightly on thy home,
Are not affection's flowers around the dome
    Entwined to make thee glad,
            O Heart,
Within the sphere where Heaven hath set thy part?

    Seek'st thou the meteor bright,
That plays awhile around the Poet's name?
Wouldst beam a star within the shrine of Fame?
    What though they gleam to-night,
            O Heart,
To-morrow's sun will see them soon depart!

If not to flame on high—
Yet thou wouldst see the Laurel on my brow,
See noble souls before the minstrel bow
　　And offer tear or sigh:
　　　　O Heart,
Could *this* allay or soothe thy secret smart?

　　Sigh'st thou for Love, fond breast?
Wouldst thou his sweet and rosy garland twine,
And lay the tribute on the flaming shrine
　　Of Hymen?—Sad unrest, ·
　　　　O Heart,
Too often is the meed of Love's flower-hidden dart!

　　Seek'st thou a kindred soul,
Whose every pulse shall vibrate with thine here?
Who'll give thee smile for smile and tear for tear?
　　Thy sure magnetic pole?—
　　　　O Heart,
Friendship like *this* has not on earth a part?

　　Yet cease fond Heart to sigh—
Lo! Jesus cometh with his Angels bright,
To welcome thee before the Throne of Light;
　　Beneath his beaming eye,
　　　　O Heart,
All vain desires and foolish hopes depart.

Midnight Musings.

———

I.

'Tis the noon of night—the stars are shining bright,
  Looking down upon me with their holy eyes!
Sleep has flown away—Spirit-borne I stray
  Through their realm of boundless mysteries.

Pure and solemn stars!—Nothing adverse mars
  The majestic course of their harmonious sweep—
Only one frail power—fell in evil hour,
  Over whose decline the angels weep!

Through the fields of air—rushing in despair,
  Plunging ever downward, darkward, more and more,
From etherial height—all bereft of light,—
  Hung eclipsed above the stygian shore!

But ETERNAL THOUGHT—its redemption wrought—
  Letting down from Heaven a pure golden chain,
Links of *Love* and *Grace*—lifting to its space,
  'Mid her sister orbs once more to reign.

II.

It is said the soul—ere it met control
  Of the earthly body, a melodious sphere,
With ærial grace—floated through all space,
  Drinking in the harmonies of air—

Neared the inner shrine—Heard the voice Divine,
  Which all other harmonies so far excel—
Made it thence *the note*—whose sweet echoes mote
  Every discord from her life expel.

We a higher flight through the realms of Light
    Take—and veering heavenward read the sacred lore;
Breath of Very God—breathed in moulded sod,
    Lit the spark that burneth evermore!

Of *so* high degree—Man must ever be
    Left with godlike license of Free Will to choose—
'Twixt the bad and good—*Husk* or *Heavenly* food—
    Light—or Darkness of cimmerian hues!

'Mid the fragrant flowers—of the Eden bowers,
    Near the fatal tree of Knowledge, Satan stood—
By his own dread might—changed to form of Light,
    "Eat belovéd, this is Angel's food."

God, who cannot lie—uttered "*Sin* and *die!*"
    Was there none on Earth to change the just decree?
From th' Eternal Dome—Lo! a voice—"I come
    For this hour has God begotten ME!"

III.

Shout redeeméd Earth—and ye souls whose birth
    To the Life immortal, brought the Son Divine
From His Father's rest—to the Virgin's breast,
    Evermore from thence a light to shine—

Filling Heaven and Earth!—Angels catch our mirth,
    Borrowed first from your seraphic natal lay,
When a stream of light—thwart the track of Night—
    Ye to Shepherds heralded THE RAY!
  8

The Lay of A Lone Heart.

SWEET is the carol of the birds
    At dewy dawn of day;
And sweet the warble of their throats
    All through the flowery May;
They sing—and never fear a rude
    Discordant note shall jar
Upon a pure refined ear
    And all the music mar.

O birds! your liquid, gushing strains
    Pour sadness on my heart;
Would that like you, in conscious power,
    I too could bear a part
In Nature's universal hymn,
    And to its Author lift
The tribute of a grateful soul,
    For a *true—perfect* gift.

But all the notes that I can frame
    Harsh, dissonant, or low,
In broken and disjointed strains,
    From a wounded spirit flow:
And yet I *feel* the gift of song
    To me *in part* is given,
But *he*, who used to set it true,
    Now swells the chant of Heaven!*

*Rev. C. Wallace, the author's friend and pastor.

He, who with tender guiding hand,
   My trembling footsteps led,
To where the Saviour's flock repose
   On fresh and verdant bed,
Fast by the Stream of Life that flowed
   In rippling murmur by,
Soothing the sorrow-stricken heart,
   And hushing every sigh!

Nor only in those pastures green,
   And by the Holy Hill;
But through the Vale of Poësy
   And by its gurgling rill
He led me—and his word of cheer
   My timid heart would fire
With hope that *even* song of mine
   Might swell the minstrel choir!

The world is full of minds of might
   God-gifted, holy, free—
But *he* is gone and none are near
   To guide and comfort me!
Alone, and groping in the dark
   I wander night and day,
And strike my rude and timid harp
   In secret, far away.

In some lone, darksome, dreary nook,
   Where none can hear my song—
O birds! would that my breast could pour
   Your *perfect* notes and *strong ;*—
Would that an *instinct* true as yours
   Could give my yearning-voice;
Then should my early, gladsome lay
   Wake Nature to rejoice.

O that the *faith* in me was strong
  To *feel my music true*,
Then should I hail the dawning light
  With carols ever new:
But no—*I cannot trust my song*,
  And none to me is given,
To fill the void in heart and life,
  Since *he* has gone to Heaven!

Autumnal Musings.

THE year is dying out—the Autumnal breeze
Sweeps o'er the forest trees,
Awaking solemn music in the heart
Attuned to bear her part
In Nature's diapason, and to hear
God's voice forever near;
    Speaking in whispers low
    When Zephyrs blow
      O'er rosy bowers;
    And when the rude winds bow
    The pines as now,
      And tempest lowers.

Now on the margin of the river
The red and golden leaflets quiver,
Ready to drop on flood or clay;
To float as fairy barks away,
    Or spread a carpet meet
    For stern December's icy feet:

Red the Sun,
His day's work done,
Seeks his crimson couch of rest
O'er Mount Kathrine's modest crest,
Without a sigh
Like him may I,
Through golden portals pass, to rise
After death's tranquil sleep, in worlds beyond the skies!

The year is dying out—may sin
Die from my soul within;
O, that the wintry winds could blow it thence!
Restore lost innocence;
Sweep clean the mansion—make my guilty soul
A fair unspotted scroll,
To write Life's deeds anew,
That they could strew
My passions on the ground
And I be found
Pure as the Lily flower
Washed by an April shower!

"Not so! Not so!
'Tis not Autumnal breezes that must blow
Athwart thy sinful breast;
Not North-winds rushing by,
Nor the South's balmy sigh
Can purge that guilty nest;
Call on the Spirit with a mighty prayer—
His kindly breath shall bear
The dew of healing to thy wounded soul,
And work a wonder by Divine control:
At his approach the fruits of virtue spring,
And odorous spices fling

Rich perfume o'er the garden of the soul ;
His influence prepare
Hymenial banquets there,
Meet for the Bridegroom when he takes his rest
In thy regenerate breast!"

List! in the cany brake,
Ærial voices make
Soft melody to lull the dying day
Passing away—away ;
And I the dying year
With kindred notes would cheer,
Now speeding to his dark and chilly grave ;
And when, like Year and Day,
I too must pass away,
May sounds angelical my spirit lave
In music's liquid tide :
And should the night-bird's scream
As now disturb my dream ;—
Or beatific visions as they glide
In golden haze before my fading sight ;—
O may its note be found
Only to throw around
A solemnized and spirit-stirring awe,
As the lone soul doth draw
Nearer the borders of the unknown land—
Where the pure white-robed band,
With flowery garlands, stand
Ready to welcome to th' Eternal Height
The ransomed of the Lord—the saved from Hell's
despite !

PART THE SECOND.

Poems, Patriotic and Elegiac,

GROWING OUT OF

THE LATE WAR.

Furl that banner—softly, slowly;
Furl it gently, it is holy,
    For it droops above the dead.
Touch it not, unfurl it never,
Let it droop there, furled forever,
    For its people's hopes are fled.
               [RYAN.

Arise!

Carolinians! who inherit
  Blood which flowed in patriot veins!
Rouse ye from lethargic slumber!
  Rouse and fling away your chains!
From the mountain to the seaboard
  Let the cry be—Up! Arise!
Throw our pure Palmetto banner
  Proudly upward to the skies.

Fling it out—its Lone Star beaming
  Brightly to the Nation's gaze—
Lo! another star arises!
  Quickly—proudly *it* emblaze—
Yet another! Bid it welcome
  With a hearty "three times three;"
Send it forth, on boom of cannon,
  Southern men will *dare* be free!

Faster than the cross of battle
  Summoned rude Clan Alpine's host;
Flash the news from sea to mountain,
  Back from mountain to the coast!
On the lightning's wing it fleeth—
  Scares the Eagle in his flight,
As his keen eye sees arising,
  Glory—yet shall daze his sight!

Cease the triumph—days of darkness
  Loom upon us from afar;
Can a woman's voice for battle
  Ring the fatal note of war?—

Yes—when we have borne aggression,
  Till submission is disgrace,
Southern women call for *action*—
  Ready would the danger face!

Yes—in many a matron's bosom
  Burns the Spartan spirit now;
From the maiden's eye it flashes,
  Glows upon her snowy brow;
E'en our infants in their prattle
  Urge us on to *risk our all;*—
" Would we leave them, as a blessing,
  The Oppressor's hateful thrall!"

No!—then up, true-hearted Southrons,
  Like bold "giants nerved by wine,"
Never fear! the cause is holy—
  It is sacred—yea Divine!
For the Lord of Hosts is with us—
  It is *He* has cast our lot;
Blest our homes—from lordly mansion,
  To the humblest negro cot.

God of Battles! hear our cry,
Give us nerve to *do* or *die!*
Charleston, November 12th, 1860.

Hymn of Freedom.

HAIL the birth of Southern Freedom!
　Hail the glorious herald star!
From the purple field of morning
　Flinging its pure sheen afar;
Brighter than the light Hyperian
　Beaming on Aurora's brow,
Shines the brilliant Orb of Freedom,
　Carolina's frontlet now!

Glorious Star! which Carolina
　Hangs a beacon to *the world;*
From its proud, exalted station
　Never more shall it be hurled!
Sister orbs *may* light their fires
　At its pure, refulgent flame,
But till Time's great torch expires,
　It shall burn fore'er the same!

Bow the knee to God eternal,
　Our Creator, Saviour, King;
Till He take us to the shelter
　Of His own Almighty Wing;
Till the unction of His Spirit,
　Rests upon our Country's shrine;
And we live, a chosen people,
　In the Light of Love Divine!
November 19th, 1860.

The Patriot Seer.

THE PATRIOT SEER.

WRITTEN AFTER READING THE HON. F. W. PICKENS' LETTER FROM
POLAND.

"Poland! Poland! we have heard thy story;
Poland's sons are Poland's glory!"

On ancient Warsaw's storied height,
    From bright Sarmatian plain,
The patriot thought upon his home
    Far o'er the western main;
From where each hoary feudal tower
    Shot upward to the sky—
Thought of his far off Southern home
    With moist, prophetic eye,
And faithful bosom all aglow,
To stand by her—come weal, come woe!

No more in half barbaric state,
    And Eastern splendor rare,
Elective nobles with their trains
    To Volo's mead repair:
No longer Poland's warriors flash
    Their free swords to the sky,
Their arms made mighty by the glance
    Of woman's kindling eye!
For Polish women ever stood
Undaunted 'mid the fiery flood!

No longer free—no longer great—
  Poland dismembered lies,
Blotted from Nations of the Earth,
  'Neath God's o'erarching skies;
Yet has *she* left a *living name*
  On Time's historic page,
Traced with a pen of light—her sons
  Eternal heritage!—
A name which thrills the patriot's soul—
He kindles at the name of—Pole!

And such as Poland was of yore,
  We Southrons are to-day—
A gallant, proud, heroic race;
  And *will* remain alway—
Holding the Land in fee of God;
  Elected, by His will,
To patriarchal rule o'er rude
  Untutored tribes—To fill,
Their minds with holy Christian lore,
They ne'er had learnt on Heathen shore!

And gallant Poland might have stood
  'Gainst leagued oppression's power,
Had her brave sons been *leal* and true
  In *her* dark trial hour;
Had her bold chiefs put local feuds,
  And jealous rancor down—
A modern halo would have ringed
  Her name of old renown;—
A people gallant, bold and free,
United ne'er can conquered be!

So mused the patriot—and sent
  That sigh upon the breeze
To where old Ocean's billows lave
  Our rough Palmetto trees—
To where his far off Southern home
  Beamed as a gem of light,—
Caught not his keen prophetic ken,
  The Lone Star—Glorious sight!
Wheeling her silver-cinctured car
Right to the front of Freedom's war!
November 23d, 1860.

Canaan's Doom.

" None can stay His hand, or say unto Him what doeth thou ?"

IT fell—the curse malign
  Upon the head of Ham ;
He cowered in amaze and fright,
  Before the great " I Am "—
As He, the Eternal God,
  Through the insulted Sire,
Hurled it upon his guilty head
  In stern, enduring ire;
And hallowed each domestic shrine,
By that awe-striking Act Divine!   [*Gen. 9th.*

And the fresh, fertile earth,
  Baptizéd by the flood,
Heard—and her bosom felt the shock
  Of severed brotherhood!

All through her forests green,
    And caverned mountains rude
Echoed the awful thunder-stroke
    Of Canaan's servitude—
" Servant of servants shall he be
To Japhet's large posterity !"

None may the curse remove—
    To last until The Day
When gathered nations of the Earth
    Must face the dreadful ray
    Of Christ the Judge—and call—
    Yea, voice of *bond* and *free*
Shall mingle in that awful cry,
    "O mountain fall on me,
And cover from the Eye of Him
Who rides upon the Cherubim !"   [*Rev. 6th*

The faithful Abraham dwelt
    Among his bondmen dear,
Those whom a righteous God had placed
    Beneath his fostering care :—
    Lo! to an aged slave
    What mighty trust is given !
" For Isaac bring the chosen bride
    Elect of Highest Heaven ;
For, from my son, it is decreed,
Shall come the holy, promised Seed."
                [*Gen. 29th.*

And when with joyous feet
    The hosts of Israel prest,
On further side of Jordan's flood
    The land of happy rest ;

And raised their altars pure
To the One holy God—
The sons of Labor dwelt with them
Upon the sacred sod;
Bearing the water and the wood,
In humble, cheerful servitude.

At last, in God's full time,
The promised Seed *was given*
And meekly Jesus walked the Earth,
So late the King of Heaven;
He who at sin could hurl
The lightning shaft of ire,
And cause his human visage glow
With Godhead's awful fire!
Would he permit His holy eye,
Rest on a crime and pass it by?

When the Centurion sought
His blessing for his slave—
" My servant is tormented sore,
Lord speak the word 'and save'"—
Christ said not—"get thee hence
And set thy bondman free,
Ere thou presume in suppliance meek
To bow the reverent knee"—
But, marvelling at his faith's great power,
Healed his sick slave " the self-same hour."

[*Matt. 8th.*

And they who read aright
The Word of God may see
How prophets, priests, apostles, all
Uphold the dread decree ;—

They have not *dared* to set
The seal of Heaven aside,
As modern fanatics would do
In bold presumptuous pride,
But urged on servants to obey—
On Masters—to bear equal sway!

See that your tents become
O Japhet! schools of Grace,
Where Gospel blessings may distill
On Canaan's humble race;
Remembering ye too have
A Master just—on high,
Who, on the Judgment morn, the works
Of *every man* shall try—
If faithful found—or bond—or free
Shall dwell with Christ Eternally!

Limerick Plantation, December 26th, 1860.

For the Germans.

Born in the year when Germans' rose
" *En masse* " to free their land,
From foreign Despot's galling yoke—
From France's iron hand!
How can I help it that my blood
Flows tingling through each vein,
My heart leaps high—my pulses throb
To snap the cord in twain
That binds us to fraternal foe,
Would work us dark, malignant woe!

When Liberty's *true sun* arose
   On Lands of old renown,
Presaging soon the meteor glare
   Of carnage should go down!
When valor bared his strong right arm,
   And flashing to the sky
The sword of Justice, called on God
   To bless it from on high!—
And God did bless it—hear Him say,
" Vengeance is mine, I will repay."

Then the immortal Korner seized
   His Country's slumbering lyre,
And ran o'er its neglected chords
   His fingers tipped with fire!—
Like him I may not dare to sing
   High pæan to the sword,
But I can kiss with glowing lip,
   And bless with holy word—
The blades—if forced to battle-field—
Our gallant sons shall bravely wield!

For in my heart I feel the glow
   Of high prophetic fires!
Great Deborah's exalted faith
   My patriot-soul inspires—
And I would make her battle-cry
   Resound throughout the land—
" Up, for the day of God has come,
   Deliverance is at hand!
Up!—lest the curse of Meroz fall!—
Ye came not at JEHOVAH's call!"

But German hearts beat warm and true
　　As when in Father-Land,
They rallied at fair Freedom's call
　　And seized the battle-brand!—
And now at Carolina's voice,
　　With hearts exultant-free—
They lock their sinewy arms around
　　Her firm Palmetto Tree!—
Strong arms! that erst Napoleon's car
Backed on his gory track of war!

November, 1860.

Forts Morris and Moultrie.

HARK the wind-storm how it rushes!—
　　List! methinks I hear the strain
Of wild music it awak'neth,
　　As it sweeps along the main!
Rustling in the old Palmettos—
　　Stirs it not each patriot breast,
In the Camp of proud Fort Morris,
　　On this day of holy rest?

Day of Rest in the good city,—
　　But *down there*, along the strand,
Active work—and keen-eyed watching
　　For the brave, heroic band,
To whom God has given honor,
　　In permitting them to be
First to send the shot for Freedom,
　　Booming o'er the foaming sea!

Soon Old Moultrie caught the signal—
　　Fort beloved of Southern heart!
And, tho' Sumter frowned defiant,
　　With loud war-note took her part;
And *those brave men never faltered,*
　　Tho' the false and craven foe
Late had sworn, "if once they opened,
　　He would lay the Fortress low!"

'Tis a tale to tell our children,
　　How we eager stood to hear
The first gun of Freedom sounding
　　Grandly, proudly on the ear!
When again our batteries open
　　Seaward on the approaching foe,
Their returning shot may bring us
　　Desolation, anguish, woe.

Yet our loved ones—wives and mothers,
　　Daughters, sisters, sweethearts stand
Ready to cheer on to glory
　　Our devoted patriot band!
Not a heart with fear is quailing;
　　Not an eye but glows with pride;
Only those are sad whose kindred
　　Still at home are forced to bide!

O, true-hearted, noble brother,
　　Now, for you and all the brave,
Will I kneel in suppliance lowly
　　To the One who died to save!
May his angels camp around ye,
　　May His shield be o'er ye thrown,
And the glory of His presence
　　All encircle as a zone.

Should ye fall, a band of martyrs,
  In the mighty cause of truth,
May the seal of the Redemption
  Stamp ye for eternal youth!
For I *know the cause is holy*,
  Not a doubt is in my soul;
And a hero is each soldier
  On our SACRED MUSTER ROLL!

Charleston, January 13th, 1861.

Sonnet.

ADDRESSED TO THE HON. R. B. RHETT.

REJOICING in our Freedom, it is meet
  We give the honor where 'tis justly due,
  And, as in antique triumphs, forth and strew
Fresh, fragrant flowers beneath the victor's feet,
And with exultant pæans loudly greet
  The faithful and undaunted. Many years
  He wrestled all alone, through hopes and fears,
His country's glorious ransom to complete.

His State may prove forgetful, and withhold
  The robes of Office—but his patriot breast
Beats 'neath a purer mantle—every fold
  Fraught with a blessing of enduring test,
The love of hearts enfranchised! All untold
  The deep serene of his well-earned rest.

January, 1861.

Greeting for Victory.

———

CAROLINIANS! ye have answered
  To our Mother's thrilling call,
And I love ye, oh! my brothers!
  Love ye dearly, one and all;
How my heart went forth rejoicing
  O'er each brave one as he flew
To the rescue of *that* Mother,
  With high hope and purpose true.

And our God has blessed us, brothers,
  Blessed our valor—blessed our cause,
In a way shall make the kingdoms
  Of the whole round world to pause,
Deep reflecting; was there ever
  Such deliverance wrought on earth—
So sublimely grand a pageant
  To announce a Nation's birth?

Most resembling war of angels
  By immortal poet sung,
Was the scene—terrific—awful—
  Now the theme of every tongue:
Carolina's bards the story
  Shall rehearse in verse sublime,
Handing down *her* name of glory
  To the very verge of Time!

Carolina!—Glorious Mother!
  First in wisdom—first in might—
Blessed be the God of Heaven,
  It was *thine* to lead the fight!

How mine eyes have ached with watching
　For the dawning of *that day ;*
It has passed—alas for hoping—
　My sad orbs drank not its ray.

As I caught the distant thunder,
　First I trembled with affright—
Then my bosom filled, triumphant
　With a strange and wild delight;
For I knew *thy sons*, my Mother,
　Would redeem thee on *that day,*
Pour their warm heart-blood, if needed,
　To enrich thy glorious way !

Carolina's sons of honor—
　Sons of glory—sons of truth,
Would not fail her in the hour
　Of her greatest need and ruth :
And the God of Battles thundered,
　Rolled His chariot through the sky—
Flashed the glory of His presence,
　As He passed majestic by.

Heard ye not the mighty rushing
　Of *His seraphs* as they threw
Their strong wings, a shield of shelter
　From the war-bolts as they flew ?
Fought *He* not with weapons tempered
　By *His justice* and *His truth*—
By the side of veteran soldiers,
　And the glowing heart of youth ?—

Honor to our chosen captains—
　To our manhood—to our youth—
To the wisdom of our Council—
　To our valor—to our truth—

To our brave hearts wildly throbbing
　For *their turn* that stirring day,
Like the anxious war-steed champing
　At the *stern fate* of delay,—

As they saw *their* dream of glory
　As a cloud-drift float afar,
Rest upon the head of brother
　Like a brightly glowing star—
Rest upon the head of brother
　Not more worthy, when all drew
From the breast of Common Mother
　The *one stream* that made them true.

Bow we all, the knee adoring,
　To Jehovah, God of Might,
Rendering *chief* to Him the glory
　As is "bounden, meet and right;"
For *His strong arm* brought salvation;
　And *His hand* the garland wrought
That adorns our Mother's forehead,
　With a glory passing thought.

April 17th, 1861.

Our Banner.

———

FLUNG TO THE BREEZE AT LIMERICK, ST. JOHN'S BERKLEY, ON
THE 11TH OF APRIL, 1861.

———

HAIL to thee bright banner!
   Floating to the sky
  Kissed by April breezes
   As they hurry by
Amid the rosy bowers of the Spring to sigh!

   On the eve of battle
   When a golden light
  Shot from western heaven
   Crowned *this* sylvan height,
Before the star of Vesper heralded the night—

   Flung we forth our banner
   With its triple bars;—
  Shedding rays of glory
   From its crown of stars
Over the purple evening, rich with crystal spars.

   Soon a sylph of Faëry
   From her silver sphere,
  Shed soft, balmy tear drops
   On our symbol fair:
Fresh from this baptism we left it floating there!

10

When our country's banner
  Next enrapt my sight,
Like a wing of glory
  It was gleaming bright
Over heaving ocean from mast and fortress height!

Soon a crimson shower
  May enrich each fold ;
And the Sun of Glory
  Shoot *his* rays of gold
Adown its borders drooping over heroes cold.

Yet we hail thee, banner!
  Blessed of Heaven—and view
With glad eyes, triumphant,
  Faith-fraught hearts—and true,
Thy bright enlarging circlet, on its shield of blue!

Hail *our own* bright banner!
  From its grassy mound
Shooting to the azure :
  While the trees around,
Fair fields, and sparkling waters seem enchanted ground!

Old Moultrie.

THE splendor falls on bannered walls
  Of ancient Moultrie, great in story;
And flushes now, his scar-seamed brow,
  With rays of golden glory!
        Great in his old renown;
        Great in the honor thrown
        Around him by the foe,
        Had sworn to lay him low!

The glory falls!—Historic walls
  Too weak to cover foes insulting;
Became a tower—a sheltering bower—
  A theme of joy exulting:
        God, merciful and great,
        Preserved the high estate
        Of Moultrie, by His power,
        Through the fierce battle hour!

The splendor fell—His banners swell
  Majestic forth to catch the shower;
Our own loved *blue* receives anew *
  A rich immortal dower!—
        Adown the triple bars
        Of its companion,† spars
        Of golden glory stream;
        On seven-rayed circlet beam!

---

*The Banner of the State.
†The Confederate Flag.

The glory falls—but not on walls
　　Of Sumter deemed "*the post of duty*,"
A brilliant sphere, it circles clear
　　The harbor in its beauty ;
　　　　　Holding in its embrace
　　　　　The city's queenly grace ;
　　　　　Stern battery and tower,
　　　　　Of manly strength and power.

But brightest falls on Moultrie's walls,
　　Forever there to rest in glory ;
A hallowed light—on buttress height—
　　O Fort, beloved and hoary !
　　　　　Rest *there*—and tell that *faith*
　　　　　Shall never suffer scath ;—
　　　　　Rest there—and glow afar
　　　　　Hope's ever-beaming star !
Charleston, May 3d, 1861.

NOTE.—All lovers of poetry will know in whose liquid gold I have
d pped my brush to illumine the picture.

A Sister's Farewell.

TO J. E. P., OF THE WASHINGTON L. I. VOLS., HAMPTON LEGION.

BROTHER ! in the strong assurance
　　That our cause is just and true ;
That the smile of Heaven is with us ;
　　Give I thee, my fond adieu—
Dearest brother ! patriot ever stern and true !

Not with wild throb, like our ardent
    Youthful heroes, is the beat
Of the martial spirit stirring
    In thy heart's profound retreat;
Years of waiting have intensified its beat!

Silently the patriot fire
    Has been smouldering in thy breast,
From gay youth to sturdy manhood;
    Now it breaketh from its rest,
Flaming upward, like a glory-lighted crest!

Till thy forehead, erst so placid,
    And thine eyes' serenest blue,
Seem enkindled with the halo
    Of its light—sublimely true
As I bade thee, tearfully, a long adieu.

Glowed it there—while in *thy bosom,*
    Whence it *thus* had flashed to light,
Were deep wells of sorrow springing
    As thou badst good-by to-night—
But *such waters* never quenched heroic light.

Deep affection, for the dear ones
    Left at home, shall make it glow
More intensely:—Brace the spirit,
    Nerve the arm—until the foe
Shrink affrighted from each God-commissioned blow!

If perchance a tear drop trembled
    On mine eyelid, 'twas not fear,
But the rush of strong emotion
    Sent it upward, hung it there,
Gladness raying from its dewy, crystal sphere.

If one moment, for the anguish,
  My brave spirit seemed to quail,
Trembling seized upon my members,
  And my brow began to pale—
O forget it! Woman's faith will never fail.

Mighty in the strong assurance
  That the God of Love will hear;
Passed the weakness of *this hour*—
  Soaring on the wing of prayer,
Soon my spirit shall surmount the realm of fear!

And mine eyeballs, God anointed,
  Bright, prophetic visions see
Of our Southern hosts returning
  Crowned with bays of victory,
Singing praises to the *One* has made us *free*.
May 31st, 1861.

Hampton Legion.

I.

Go—take thy place by Valor's side :—
  Ho, Legion! onward to the van!
And look! thou bearest a noble name,
  Prove each a noble man!

Revere thy banner—it was wrought
  By daughters of heroic sires ;—
The hand of beauty swiftly flew,
While tear drops moistened eyes of blue,
Or quenched in orbs of darker hue
  Their more vehement fires :

Revere it—woman's snowy breast,
Vibrating with a strange unrest
        Of hope and fear for thee,
Sent many a stifled sigh, prayer fraught,
Upward upon the wing of thought
        As grew the tapistry!
Go—beat back those whose rallying cry
Insults our Southern chastity!

Our own great Davis first unfurled
        Its beauties to thine ardent gaze;
Go—let the name beneath it won
        Fill nations with amaze!—
Bear it into the hottest fight,
Where freemen battle for their right,
Nor fear the hordes of Northern might!
And may its crescent's silvery sheen
Thy beacon be—its Palm—thy screen!

Pass on—by Hampton led—and he
Who wrestled for the civic crown
With Rhett and Pickens: Great renown
Under such chieftains mayest thou win;
Go—teach the hoary man of sin
Thy prowess!   Let each belted knight,
And every warrior of the host,
As he assumes his sacred post,
Feel he commission bears to fight
For Home and Liberty!

Press on—encompassed as thou art
By prayers from woman's loving heart!
Nor deem these sacred fires shall die;
In circling wreaths they mount the sky,
Fanned by the breath of Love and Faith's reviving sigh!

II.

Thus sung I ere in Piedmont's vale
The battle din had filled the gale;
Or Sabbath sunlight hailed the dawn
And life-throe of a nation born
  In agony and blood!
Ere yet the thrilling news had sped
That told of mighty armies fled—
And foes all gory, cold and dead
  Upon Manassas' plain!
That told how freemen nobly fought,
And countless deeds of valor wrought;
Deeds of surpassing valor, fraught
  With light of Chivalry!
The old historic war-harp blends
Its music with the shout that rends
  The air for Victory!

Great Bee and Bartow grandly died—
Pure Johnson fell—The Legion's pride,
Struck down at noble Hampton's side
  At opening of the fray,
Ere his heroic spirit caught
The thrill of triumph—or was fraught
With grateful homage at the thought
  Of Freedom's dawning day!

O Legion! O heroic band!
Soul-strengthened by thy God to stand
  Unflinching 'mid the storm;
A greater bard than I thy praise
Shall hand far down the golden days
  That yet shall bless our land!

A prouder and a sweeter strain
Than any I can 'wake, thy slain
  Must lull to their repose!—
Mine be the thrilling note of war!
Ho, Southrons! every one prepare—
  Avenge the noble dead!
Great Georgia bares her bleeding breast—
Virginia sets her spear in rest,
  And waits another blow;
Let every Southron don his mail,
And like the war-steed snuff the gale,
  Then rush upon the foe!
Go take *his place* by heroes' side,
And where the war-nooks open wide
  Step in with dauntless tread!

Baptizéd for the dead—go then,
A band of Heaven-anointed men,
  And fill our vacant flanks—
As in the early Days of Grace,
The Christian warriors filled each space
  Cleft in their martyr ranks;
So may confessors for *our creed*,
By thousands from its blood-red seed
Spring for their country's *now*, as *then* the Church's need.
 Charleston, August 3d, 1861.
  11

Strike the Harp.

A HYMN OF PRAISE FOR A BROTHER'S SAFETY AT "THE BATTLE
OF MANASSAS," SUNDAY, JULY 21ST, 1861.

STRIKE the harp to God Eternal;
   Strike the harp of sweetest string;
With a song of holy triumph
   Let the Southern welkin ring!
Let the women and the children
   To their household altars hie,
And around their sacred fires
   Chant the song of Victory!

Let each bosom bring the gladness,
   Or the sorrow if it be—
For alas! our hymn of triumph
   Chimes no bloodless victory—
Let it all be humbly offered
   To our Saviour and our God,
That the hand of Love and Mercy
   May remove the chastening rod.

God, I thank Thee for the answer
   Thou hast granted to my prayer;
For the shield of Thy protection
   Thrown above my brother dear:
By thy strong right arm supported
   Safely through the storm he passed,
While brave comrades fell around him,
   Stricken by the battle blast.

In the fore-front of the battle,
   Where the valiant fought, he stood,
Where the slaughter and the carnage
   Rolled a horrid red-sea flood!
Swift the hot bolts flew around him—
   But protected by Thy might,
Father! he has passed uninjured
   Through the sharp and deadly fight.

God, I thank thee for the calmness
   Thou imparted'st to his breast,
Filling it with holy purpose
   Nobly *there*, to do his best—
To uphold the cause of Freedom,
   Constitution, Honor, Truth—
With the valor of his manhood—
   With the yet warm fire of youth.

Kindling then with deep emotions,
   Let his kindred offer praise;
Pour out floods of grateful feeling
   To the *One* of Ancient Days;
Let us each with hearts adoring
   Bow before the Throne of Love,
And our *own* peculiar blessing
   Waft, on prayerful sigh, above!

O may this, so great salvation,
   Thrill each heart, and fill each eye;
Till with one great voice the nation
   Render God the Victory!
Till we own, with faith adoring,
   Thee, the mighty Lord of Hosts,
As the God of our redemption;
   Father, Son and Holy Ghost.

August 4th, 1861.

Daughters of the Southern Queen.

AGED mothers of our city,
  Matrons in the pride of life;
Maidens, like fair roses glowing
  In our sunny bowers; and wife,
Newly led from holy altar
  Where you gave the plighted vow,
With the orange-blossoms trembling
  Yet, above your virgin brow:
Hear ye not the wild-waves surging
  Onward in their awful roar?
God!—the foemen are upon us!—
  Hark! their footsteps tread our shore!

Long the warder* from the tower
  Shouted "danger is anear"—
But we passed on careless—reckless—
  Turning all a deafened ear:
And our leaders dreamed "the cowards
  Would not brave our arméd host!"—
Lo! their ships in countless numbers
  Thunder now along the coast!
Charleston!—Bright and peerless city
  Our own darling, joy and pride!
Is it true the fierce invader
  Comes against thee, as a tide
Of polluted waters, rushing—
  Dashing onward to defile
Carolina's fairest daughter
  And her agony revile?

* Charleston Mercury.

They have broke upon our threshold,
   And our braves *as rock* have stood,
Firm—undaunted in their spirit
   And received the tainted flood :
Fierce it came—and hot its fury,
   Heated with the breath of Hell—
Dashed in madness o'er their bosoms—
   'Neath the shock our heroes fell.

Fell—but left a name undying—
   Let us drop a sacred tear
On their cold and mangled corses
   Ere our war-cry rend the air—
" By Port Royal! to avenge them now we swear."

O! not yet our queenly city
   Shalt thou totter to thy fall,
For our bravest and our dearest
   Form around a living wall :
And with arms close locked, and bosoms
   Bared will meet the insulting foe,
Perish all ere foul dishonor
   Cause thy matron cheek to glow!

Sisters! 'tis no wild alarum
   I am sounding in your ear ;
I would draw ye by my spirit
   'Bove the tide mark of despair :
I would banish from your bosoms
   Every thought could make ye—*pale ;*
What! would let the vile intruder
   Deem that Southern women quail!

No by Heaven!   A sign of weakness
  Must not rest on cheek or brow,
Let the falling drops of anguish
  Turn to sparks of fiery glow!
Show no fear—but all in meekness
  Seek the Temple of your God—
Low before his footstool kneeling
  Kiss the hand that bares the rod;
Bow your hearts, until He answers
  With a smile shall part the shroud,
Whence the Light of Heaven streaming
  Gilds the fringes of the cloud.
November 12th, 1861.

"Die Here."

DEDICATED TO THE ARMY OF THE CONFEDERATE STATES

"IF we determine to die here"—
Thus rang the words in accents clear
From lips of the heroic Bee,
The flower of Southern chivalry!—
"Lo! Jackson like a Stonewall stands—
Come on, once more, my trusty bands,
Whom only numbers could force back
From the blood-marked, immortal track,
Where hundreds fell beneath thy stroke,
And with sharp cries of anguish 'woke
The echoes of the battle plain;—
Come on, brave Comrades! once again—
If we determine to *die here*
  We conquer—let us on—and dare."

O that these words were graven deep
On every Southern heart! I weep
To see how oft we retrograde,
When glorious stand had sure been made
Had we heroic souls. DIE HERE—
It is the *only way* whene'er
We meet the proud, insulting hate
Of foes vindictive ;—Bide our fate,
Yea, spring to it with hearts of fire,
And trust in God—He will inspire
Our patriot souls—and tho' we lie
Stiff on the bloody field—*His eye*
Shall beam approval from on High!

Here—while a mother's blessing rests
Dove-like upon our manly breasts—
While wife's embrace—or sister's tear—
Or daughter's love—or maiden's—dear,
Far dearer than a daughter's—cling
And cluster round our hearts, and bring
Sweet memories of home—and sound
Of merry laughter floats around
As from our little ones—*strike free*,
And fling the battle-cry of Bee
Up to the welkin—and the Heavenly sphere,
Shall echo back the glorious words—*Die Here !*

March 22d, 1862.

The Fairy Festival.

DEDICATED TO THE FAIR VOCALISTS OF THE CONCERT.*

WHAT magic scene is here !
Bellona can the waving of *thy* spear
Call up enchantment on the field of Death ?
    Fling o'er the blood-stained heath
Garlands of beauty ?—bid the clarion note
      Of war afar to float,
      And sweet aërial measure
      Fill every heart with pleasure ?
        Lo ! forms of fairy
Come tripping in with motion airy,
      And part to left and right,
      Fair girlhood ! bright
With promise of the glorious days to be,
When Carolina, great in Liberty,
      Shall send her name afar,
And for the darkened world the gate of light unbar !

Bright flowers are these, and jewels which our Queen
Wears not on robes of State, but near her heart ;
Not to be plucked from thence by hand of war,
And weeping captives led behind the conqueror's car !

    Now one by one three half-blown roses rise
      And charm our eager eyes :
    Can Northern gardens show such lovely flowers
      As these, by silvery showers

---

* Given in aid of the building of a gunboat for the protection of
Charleston.

And golden sun-shafts drawn
From bosom of the fair and fragrant South?
  Hark! from each rose is heard,
  The voice as of a bird!
One singing forth in gladness—one in woe
With plaint note, sweet and low;
One rousing us to deeds of high emprise,
Worthy to win a smile from those sweet loving eyes!

  The first rose flung a joy
From her pure heart, in which was no alloy
Of pain and sadness—with a careless glee,
As glad child singing by its mother's knee,
Gushed forth the witching richness of each note
    Upon the air to float,
And find its way to every worthy soul
    In reach of its control;—
God-gifted! may her heart be ever clear,
And mount as it does now towards the heavenly sphere!

  The second fairy flower
  Bore from her natal bower
A sister bud, aye clinging to her side;
  Each of their homes the pride—
  Where culture rich and rare
  Had blessed these blossoms fair,
Making them meet to bear their gifted part
    In festival of art,
And altar of their bleeding country dower
  · With perfume from their bower!—
  From heart of this fair rose,
  A thrill of pain—and throes

As from the bosom of a great despair—
   Not *thine* be fate so drear—
But guardian spirits ward each shaft of pain,
And on thy earthly path celestial blessings rain!

   The third rose springs to view!
   La Sylphide! with the morning dew
   Still clinging to her silken vest!
Can the heroic muse find fitting nest
   In that soft, fragrant breast!—
   She sings—the spirit of her race
Glows in the blushing beauty of her face;
   Speaks in her dewy eyes,
Lifted in holy fervor to the skies
   In prayer for our loved land;
And that old kingly anthem—holy, grand—
Has kept a mighty nation—faithful—true,
Thrilled to our heart of hearts and nerved our souls
   anew!

   And France's hot war note
   From clarion wont to float,
Stirring the heart to madness;—music-fire,
Setting the soul aflame with wrathful ire—
   Came tempered of its heat,
   And made an anthem meet
For our most holy cause—as from her throat
Poured the rich treasure of each stirring note,
Calling the brave to arms! God grant that *they*
Take fire from that young heart and instantly obey.
Charleston, March 24th, 1862.

Sonnet.

ADDRESSED TO JAMES SIMONS, ESQ., ON HIS COMPLIMENTING THE
AUTHOR OF THE FAIRY FESTIVAL WITH CHAUCER'S " CANTER-
BURY TALES."

THE father of sweet Poësy to me!—
To me—who hardly deem myself his child,
But some rude changeling chanting on the wild
Where *he* has dropped a bud. Not given free
To rove his garden with the honey bee,
Or ravished butterfly! like them beguiled
From odorous flower to flower; but sad exiled
From where the warbling birds hold jubilee.—
Gift, more inspiring to my timid note
Than the soft breath of Spring perfumed with flowers,
Or the rich gush of melody afloat
Upon the sunny air, while joyous hours
Haste on with winged feet to where the mote
Sports in the sunbeam of the Summer bowers.

"A Swell of Music."

ADDRESSED TO PAUL H. HAYNE, AFTER READING HIS BEAUTIFUL
POEM " MY MOTHER LAND."

A SWELL of music from the grand old sea!—
O what a thrill of joy it sent through me
As it went sweeping by!—As when we lave
Our bodies in old Ocean's tide, the wave

Braces and thrills as it breaks o'er our head;
Whilst we expect another half in dread,
Half mad with wild delight—O thus to me
Comes up this mystic music from the sea!*

Night after night from out my eastern bower
    When stormy tempests lower;
      And when the sea
Lies charmed beneath the moon's soft witchery,
Have I leant forth to meet it; and it seems
Whether borne on by storm-wing, or the beams
Of silvery moonlight, to float up from where
Proud Sumter lifts his grand, defiant head
      From Ocean's dark, deep bed,
Filling the watching foe with a vague, secret dread.

Is some prophetic bard enchained there
Wild; old-world music in him? On his brow
Wearing the classic laurel, even now,
In this degenerate age?   List to *that* strain
As it rolls onward with its rich refrain,
"My Mother Land"—Sure it should stir each breast
To noble daring—rouse from sluggard sleep
Each laggard son, causing him set in rest
    His burnished spear
    And for *that* mother dear
Do battle to the death—or ere she weep
Over their degradation, and her fall
    Beneath the Northern thrall.

    "My Mother Land,"
      Strain wild and grand,
Sweep on—from ocean bright to mountain hoary,
Till every heart throbs to the theme of glory;

*Mr. Hayne was on duty at Fort Sumter.

And patriot choirs
Chant the great deeds of their heroic sires!
· *Then* "Mother Land"
Shall see her heroes, one vast, serried band,
Drive the insulting host,
Now spread along her coast,
Down to the depths of the devouring sea,
Whose floods will lift their voice and shout forth Victory!

Sonnet.

TO PAUL H. HAYNE.

MUSIC as from the bosom of the sea!
With what a solemn and mysterious sweep
It booms up from old Ocean! I could weep,
But that the strain majestic seems to free
The spirit from all weakness. A music key
Struck near some instrument awakes a sound
Of kindred harmony, thus the rebound
From our charmed hearts with those grand notes agree.
True minstrel! pure from every envious strain
That sullies meaner souls! Still strike thy lyre,
And send its notes triumphant o'er the main,
To make each faltering, timid heart aspire
And throb for mighty deeds. Thy thrilling strain
Methinks might set the coldest breast on fire.

The Lenten Fast of 1862.

———

PUBLISHED TO AID IN THE PURCHASE OF BIBLES, PRAYER BOOKS
AND TRACTS FOR THE CONFEDERATE SOLDIERS.

———

IT is the solemn season when the Church
Puts off her beauteous garments, and with head
Bowed as a bulrush, weeps her sins, and calls
Unto her children to come up and keep
The Holy Convocation; day by day,
Before the Mercy Seat, tell out their sins,
With fasting, and with weeping, and with sighs:
To rend their hearts, and not their garbs, and turn
To the most gracious and long-suffering God,
Who throned upon the circle of the Earth,
In awful state immutable, yet hears
And turns Him to His people and *repents*,
Leaving a *blessing* where he vowed a *curse!*
No mortal intellect, however vast
Its compass and expansion, can make clear
And bring to light the hidden things of God;
No mortal eye reach this mysterious height,
How the Unchangeable keeps His decree,
Yet rolls away His judgment at our prayers.

But hark! methinks the trumpet sends a call
More solemn than 'twas wont.   The women troop
By crowds into the Temple, and bow down
With an unusual reverence—every heart
Seems ladened with a sorrow—every face

Wears on its front a coronal of pain
With resolution to endure the sting.
And here and there a venerable head
Bows his time-silvered locks before his God,
And from his heart sends up a cry for help.

The Priests before the Altar stand and weep,
Assailing Heaven with unwonted force—
"Lord spare Thy people, give not to reproach
This, Thine inheritance—To vandal rule
Give them not Father! lest the nations say
Where, where their God—and think that they are made
The refuse, and off-scouring of the earth!
This Church and People humbly kneel and cry—
Accept of their contrition—hear them Lord!
O, Thou who wept o'er Salem plead for us!
Now weeping for our country bathed in blood,
And hedged about by the exultant foe!
Stir up thy strength Jehovah, come and help,
We put our trust entirely in Thee—
Bare Thy right arm—and let Thine angel guard
Keep watch and ward around our peaceful homes;
Humbly we look up, Father, unto Thee,
And say that we have done these men no wrong—
Take Thou our righteous cause into Thy hand
And judge between us—let the Kingdoms see
That the Almighty is the God of Truth :
We ask it not for merit of our own,
For we are weak and erring—prone to sin—
But for the sake of Thine Anointed One—
Our High Priest and Redeemer—Christ the Lord!"

Then take the Ministers the Book of God,
And from that sacred treasury bring forth

Things, new and old, to strengthen and refresh;
And by their holy counsel and their faith,
Make firm our hope, and tell us where to look,
In this our day of darkness, for *the Light.*

O fainting heart! O wavering, doubting faith!
Up to the Temple and find comfort there!

Thus weeps the Church and Nation—closer we
Draw, in the inner chamber of our souls,
To our Redeemer—and like Mary sit
In humble resignation at His feet,
To catch His words of comfort and of love.
Or nearer yet with the Beloved one rest
Upon the bosom of the Son of Man
Our aching brow, and hear the great life throb
Of His true, human heart! Or, in *this storm*—
From off this heaving and tempestuous sea,
Whence we to Him are calling in affright—
Like Peter take the offered hand and feel
The warm, strong pressure of His friendly grasp
Drawing us from the billow—with him own
The present God in the still, sudden calm.

O let us lay our bosoms bare to One
Who was in all points tempted like to us,
Yet without taint of sin: The man of grief
Will catch our tears and offer them on High,
All mingled with His blood. Our earnest prayers
Within His censer thrown our Great High Priest
Shall wave before the Mercy Seat, and fling
The fragrance of their incense up to God!

We are indeed encircled by a flame
As fiery as the tongues that lapped around

The children in the furnace! May the One,
Like to the Son of God be with us there;—
Then, "the moist whistling wind" shall softly blow,
And temper so the heat that we shall chant
Like them our song of triumph—and call on
The Universe to magnify our Lord!

Like Esther's people we have been consigned
And given up to Death, but let us draw
With "humble boldness" near our King, and He
Shall tender to us the sceptre of His grace,
Filling our hearts with confidence and hope;
And tho' we must stand firm, and *fight for life*,
Yet will He bless the issue—and then comes
Our day of triumph—and our feast of Joy!

Alarum.

"The cry is still they come."

'TIS borne upon the Southern breeze
  "The foe! the foe! they come"—
It surges through the forest trees—
  And in the city's hum
It mingles with the voice of trade;
  And e'en the sacred Fane
Where we bow down to worship God
  Prolongs the startling strain.

The startling strain—Our women weep
　　And wring their hands in fear ;
And e'en our sturdy-hearted men
　　Seem bowed with anxious care :—
O ye, whose dearest have gone forth
　　To meet the battle shock,
Hie to the sheltering wing outspread
　　And to the riven Rock.

Nor deem that I have none to lose
　　In this soul-stirring strife,
Because I lack the sacred names
　　Of Mother and of wife!—
Not high upon the roll of Fame
　　Are *they*, my darling ones,
Yet Carolina owns them all
　　As her devoted sons!

One is a brother dear as life,
　　No craven soul bears he—
One *almost* as a brother dear,
　　With youthful comrades three ;
These all on old Virginia's soil
　　Wait, harnessed in the field,
"Sic semper" have they each engraved
　　Upon his burnished shield.

And I have those grown as sons
　　Beneath my maiden ken,
To the bright flush of youthful hope,
　　And prime estate of men ;
And *one* whom we can scarce restrain
　　From gory battle-field ;
These all our own Palmetto bear-
　　Emblazoned on their shield !

Then shout " Noli me tangere "
   Tho' we be forced to hie
To covert of our mountain caves,
   And lowland swamps—or die—
Yea die—before we dare disgrace
   The motto of our shield,
Or more of Carolina's soil
   As bloodless trophy yield—

To vandals, who already have
   Too firm a footing *here:*—
O give us strength Almighty One
   To conquer;—Father spare
This city where the light of Truth
   First beamed a beacon ray;
Let not *that light* go down in night,
   But glow to perfect day.

Charleston, 30th April, 1862.

A Sister's Thanksgiving.

AFTER THE BATTLE OF SEVEN PINES.

ONCE again with heart adoring
   Would I bow before thy throne
Dread Jehovah!   God of Battles,
   And Thy sovereign Mercy own;
     Thou hast saved him,
Saved my brother—thou alone!

Through the forest, in the gloaming,
  To the charge the Legion sped,
With a shout that waked the echoes
  To wild music overhead—
    Back recoiling,
  Left they many a warrior dead.

For the foe was strongly posted,
  And the night came on apace,
O for one more hour of sunlight!
  O for one short hour of grace!
    But no Joshua
  Sought *for them* Jehovah's face.

Fierce again they charge—the Legion!*
  Soon its bravest stricken lie ;—
At thy side a loved companion†
  Gave a low pathetic sigh,
    Ere his spirit
  Mounted to its native sky.

Just before his voice heroic
  Had been cheering on the fight,
Now no more the din of battle
  Reaches where his soul, in light,
    Rests forever
  In the Saviour's loving sight.

God, who took thy youthful comrade,
  Spared thee brother—spread His shield
O'er thy head again in battle
  As on hot Manassas' field :—
    Heart adore Him,
  And thy grateful tribute yield.

---

* Hampton's. † Richard Yeadon, Jr.

Yet withal rejoice with trembling
  For through many a bloody fight
Must thy dear one pass, or ever
  He rejoice thy longing sight;
    Sigh submissive,
  "God, Thou doest all things right."
Charleston, June 9th, 1862.

Youthful Heroes.

LINES SUGGESTED BY THE LAMENTED DEATH OF LIEUTENANT
J. E. M'PHERSON WASHINGTON.

War has its horrors :—but as well
It has its glorious tales to tell,
Which cause our bosoms thrill and swell.

How many would have toiled for aye
To Life's last dim, allotted day,
Without *one deed* to mark their way—

But for the clarion blast that flew,
From seaboard to our mountains blue,
Calling upon the brave and true—

To arm them in defence of right,
Their sacred homes—their altars bright
With fires from God's most Holy Height.

Our plodding men of middle age
Dreamed not to live in History's page,
Or leave a golden heritage !

How many youths of noble name
Lived in the glory of the same ;
Mere copies in the antique frame.

Now very boys start up to greet
War's mighty presence ; and with feet
That should have sought their mother—meet

Grim Death on battle-field—and go,
Strengthened by Freedom's generous glow,
Exulting forth to brave the foe.

And thou wert young—yet of an age
By Eutaw's streaming light, to gage
Thy life against fanatic rage !

And Nature in heroic mould
Had cast thy brave and ardent soul,
Too soon, alas ! to reach its goal.

Too soon for Love—but not for Fame,
Already had its loud proclaim
Gone forth, " He gilds a noble name."

O gallant youth ! We sow in grief,
Yet after waiting-season brief—
Shall wave on high the golden sheaf !

Affection waters with her tear,
The laurels on thy youthful bier,
And binds the rose of promise there !

In the fair Land beyond the gloom,
Thy spirit in immortal bloom,
Awaits its partner from the tomb.

There too thy mother to her heart
Shall fold her loved one, ne'er to part;
And Gilead's balm heal every smart!
Charleston, September 9th, 1861.

In Memory of Richard Yeadon, Jr.

WHO FELL AT THE BATTLE OF SEVEN PINES, MAY 31, 1862.

FATHER! while other hearts are wrung,
Mine is but slightly touched with pain—
What shall I render for the love
    Has visited again?
The tear of gratitude—then turn
To those whose bosoms sadly yearn
O'er loved ones they no more shall see,
And prove my heartfelt thanks to Thee
By acts of tender sympathy.

Ah! there are eyes that weep for *one*
Whose future seemed traced out in light;—
That glow of promise faded soon,
    And vanished into night.
As when from bower of the morn
The Sun shoots forth his golden horn,
And gives us earnest of a day
Shall send rejoicing on their way
Earth's weary pilgrims—then arise
Clouds that obscure him from our eyes;
Thus thine uprising, and thy fate,
O brave, ingenuous youth! who late

Shed life and light on all around,
On dreary march, or camping bound,
And in the hearts of tent-mates brave
Kindled a flame of love shall burn beyond the grave!

But is the sun forever gone
When dreary clouds obscure his beaming?
No—he burns on behind the veil—
And from *beyond* thy soul is streaming
Bright rays of promise and of peace—
And those rich rays shall ne'er decrease,
But brighten and expand—and glow
Forever in that realm where woe
Comes not—where there is no more night;
But Christ and His redeemed give Light.

Heroic youth!   He gave his life
An offering to his country's shrine—
Then let us drop the note of woe
          And rose and laurel twine
Into a garland shall express
His chivalry and tenderness!

All day the battle raged—and now
Soft twilight falls on wood and field—
But bloodier work must yet be done,
          Yon battery must yield!
"Charge, Legion, through the forest drear"—
The chieftain's words drew forth responsive cheer on
     cheer!

Urging his comrades to the fight
His voice rang silvery and clear,
And mingled with the din of war—
          And on the evening air
Floated—until a gentle sigh
Hushed it in a profound—"Good-by."

Farewell! Though it may not be ours
To deck thy bier with fragrant flowers;
Or e'en to know thy place of rest
In the great Mother's silent breast;
Or ever see the budding grass
Waved by Spring breezes as they pass
Over thy rustic grave—or hear
The wild birds singing sweetly there:
Yet leave we trustingly to God
Thy mortal part—until the sod
Gives up its dead—then with a glow
More beautiful than battle fire,
Shalt thou spring forth, and join the choir
Of martyrs who rejoicing go,
Where sits the Prince of Peace upon His throne;
Where sound of war shall cease, and sorrow be unknown!

Sonnet.

DEDICATED TO THE MEMORY OF SERGEANT HAMETT, OF HAMPTON
LEGION, WHO FELL IN THE BATTLE OF THE SEVEN PINES.

KIND, unknown Friend!—and thou too in the wood
Of Chickahominy gave up thy life;
A hero Martyr in the sacred strife
For Freedom! Tidings sad and rude
To fall on loving hearts that daily brood
Over thy long, long absence. One afar
Sheds silent sorrowing tears for *thee*—the star
Struck from *their* firmament. Thy generous mood,

13

From ample garner of thy noble breast,
Gave with no stinted measure words to cheer
A heart too often troubled with unrest,
To find its music, floating on the air,
Wake no harmonic chord.   O grief oppressed!
That heart shall miss the orb that lit thy sphere.

A Chaplet.

FOR THE GRAVE OF EDWARD MYDDLETON GOODWYN.   ALL SAINT'S
DAY, NOVEMBER 1, 1862.

HEART cheering morn! affection's tear
Glows with a radiance heavenly clear
To hail thy dawning!   Saints below
Commune with those above—and go
To deck their graves with flowers!   *Here*
A garland of rich hues—and *there*
One of white rosebuds—there again
A fair lone blossom, moist with rain
From a fond, broken heart.   The air
Seems fragrant with the breath of prayer,
Floating towards the golden sphere,
To mingle with the songs that rise
Forever from that Paradise,
Where spirits of our loved are winging
Their happy flight, and earthward flinging
Some fragments of the rapturous joy
Filling their blood-washed souls with bliss beyond alloy!

And thou art with them, noble boy!
The loved of many hearts, the joy
And sun of the home-circle, where
Thy stricken parents bend in prayer
    For strength to bear the blow
    That laid their darling low;
      Yea, Grace to bear
      The threefold blast
That o'er their Eden passed
And stripped it of its blossoms—leaving drear
    A region erst so fair!
Two have been gathered unto sweet repose
Where the warm Southern sun his radiance throws
Full on their couches—while 'neath Western skies
Another calmly sleeps till God shall bid him rise!

    I have no cherished bud to lay,
    Bright youth! upon thy bed of clay—
    The garden walk is far away
    Where last we parted; and I brought
    No flowerets thence but those of thought
    And memory, which now I weave
    Into a chaplet rude, and leave
    To perish on thy grave. The flower
    I gave thee in that parting hour
    Long since has withered. Emblem meet
    Of thine own passage, bright and fleet
From beauty to decay;—Where now the hope
    That thy life's bud would bloom and ope
Into a perfect flower! The rainbow dream
    That saw thy noon of manhood beam
With light of genius, latent in thine eye
Then veiled with drooping lash and adolescence shy.

Our wish for thee was earthly fame—
God traced, with pen of light, thy name
Within the Book of Life, and there
Set to His seal—"Salvation's heir!"—
O Love, surpassing mortal thought!—
O wonder of redemption, wrought
By the Eternal Son and brought
Home to the soul by influence sweet
Of the life-giving Paraclete!
Cease sorrowing tears, O cease to flow!
Change, change our suppliant notes of woe
To songs of triumph! Let our joy abound,
For this our precious one, searched out and found
By the good Shepherd, and upon His breast
Borne to His Father's home—*the* fold of *Heavenly* Rest.

The Standard-Bearer.

Written when in anxious suspense as to the fate of Charles Bernard Foster, who was wounded in the engagement on the Weldon and Petersburg Railroad, on the 21st of August, 1864, while carrying the "colors" of his regiment, the Twenty-seventh S. C. V.

It is a strange coincidence that these lines were composed the day of his death, September 17th, 1864.

SAY didst thou bear them proudly boy
All through the deadly fray,
Without *one* quiver of affright
Or waver of dismay!—

Calmly and bravely pressing on
  Through the dense fiery hail,
As if thy form had been encased
  In panoply of mail!

"The Colors" waving o'er thy head;
  Thy grey eye lit with ire,
As when the Eagle concentrates
  Within his orb the fire,
That burns within his eager breast
  When an *intruder* dares
To scale his eyrie's peaceful height,
  His *home* of hopes and cares.

If so, I cannot weep thy fate,
  But gladly cry "well done"
Thou darling of my yearning heart—
  My sister's first-born son!
"Well done"—tho' death should be the meed
  Attendant on thy fall—
No gentle spirit hovering near—
  No Mother at thy call.   .

We know how cool and calmly thou
  Hast stood in many a fight;
And when those deadly shells were hurled
  At Sumter's crumbling height,
How, with heroic comrades three,
  Thou stoodst unshaken *there,*
And nailed the banner to the staff
  While Ocean caught the cheer—

That from exultant hearts went up
  In chorus bold and free,
As once again the starry cross
  Waved proudly o'er the sea;

How—as the curling smoke-wreaths part
  And show the dauntless band,*
Admiring comrades flung the shout
  Resounding to the land!

Ah me! the heroic thrill is past—
  My woman's heart once more,
Sinks—as a wrecked hope drifted up
  And stranded on the shore—
Into the yielding sands of Care,
  Where moaning night-winds sigh,
And Ocean's verberating boom
  Sounds on Eternally!

For none can tell us of thy fate—
  None know if Life or Death,
Or, warms thee with its genial heat,
  Or, chills with icy breath!
If still thy guileless, loving heart
  In languishment beats on;
Or, thy freed spirit floats in light
  Above the starry zone!

None know—Submissively we bow
  To kiss the chastening rod;—
Remove, in thy good time, the cloud
  That veils *his* fate O God!
Pour light though it be but to show
  Him lost forever here; .
Remove the darkness and the doubt—
  The ebbing Hope and Fear.

---

* NOTE.—James Tupper, who first saw the fall of the banner, and flew
to its rescue, assisted by C. B. Foster, W. C. Buckheister and A. J. Bluett,
all of the Twenty-seventh Regiment, S. C. V., commanded by Colonel
Gaillard.

A Farewell,

TO A YOUTHFUL SOLDIER ON HIS EIGHTEENTH BIRTHDAY, OCTOBER
12TH, 1864.

FAREWELL dear Harry, once again
   Thou goest to meet the foe,
On Old Virginia's blood-soaked plains
   And valleys, where the low
And plaintive note of woman's wail
With strains æolian fill the gale,
And ghosts of heroes wander pale
   And beckon to the fight.

Go—for behold the rose of health
   Is blushing on thy cheek;
And pulses that a month ago
   Were languishingly weak,
Now with a full and vigorous beat,
Tell that the warm blood courses fleet,
Through artery and vein, to greet
   The heart's new throb of Life.

No longer from thy lip and brow
   We wipe the beaded dew;
The love-light sparkles yet again
   Within thine eye of blue;
Thy wounds all healed, thy fever fled,
Firm and elastic falls thy tread,
We would not keep thee here tho' dread
   Attends the parting hour.

For mourn we not thy brother Charles
　　Now held in captive thrall,
Without one kindred spirit near
　　To heed his plaintive call;
Shorn of a limb he bleeding lies,
The pain-film dimming his dear eyes,
No loved one by to sympathize,
　　Or wipe his clammy brow !

Let not his mournful fate appal—
　　Thy Country needs thine arm;
And may thy mother's God, and mine
　　Keep thee from every harm;
In battle's fierce and fiery hour
Be thy protecting shield and tower;
In loathsome trench a sheltering bower
　╲ Above thy youthful head!

Go—and aquit thee as before,
　　Shame *men* who keep away;
Thou brave *boy-veteran* whose years
　　Cycle *eighteen* to-day !—
And may the Everlasting Arm,
Encircling, shield from every harm;
God's Pure and holy spirit calm
　　And hallow this farewell.

The Pure-Hearted.

Dedicated to the memory of the friends and cousins Isaac Ball Gibbs and Charles Bernard Foster, who received their death wounds in the bloody fight on the Weldon and Petersburg Railroad, on the 21st of August, 1864, members of Hagood's Brigade, which suffered so terribly on that fatal field.

I. B. Gibbs, of Company B, Twenty-fifth Regiment S. C. V., after hours of intense agony, is supposed to have expired during the night—exchanging the toil and turmoil of war for a glorious eternity. A true soldier of the Cross and of his country; he died in his 24th year, leaving the odor of a good name and a life of sanctity.

C. B. Foster, of Company D, Twenty-seventh Regiment S. C. V., after passing unscathed through many battles, in all of which he had been noted for coolness and intrepidity, while gallantly bearing the "colors" of his regiment, on the eventful 21st of August, FELL wounded in the wrist and foot; and after suffering amputation of the latter and enduring weeks of anguish, expired at the Sickles Hospital, Alexandria, Virginia, on the 17th of September, aged 21 years, 10 months and 4 days. "Loveable and full of promise," his pure and guileless spirit passed from the bed of suffering to the bosom of his God.

> " Lovely and pleasant in their lives ;"
> In their death they were not divided.

JESUS, The Word Divine, has said
   The pure in heart shall see
The beauty of His Father's face,
   Its glorious majesty :
And who so pure, so free from stain
As *these*, whose memories remain
As precious perfume poured around,
To bless and sanctify the ground
Where their beloved forms shall nevermore be found !

" Lovely and pleasant in their lives "—
  Kindred in *blood* and *thought*,
None with a more heroic zeal
  Freedom's stern battle fought :
The dreary march, the loathsome trench,
Disease and hunger, naught could quench
The patriotic fire that grew
Intensely in their hearts, and threw
A glow and warmth around which kept the wavering
  true.

With minds contemplative and grave
  They loved, in classic bower,
With sages of the mighty Past
  To commune hour by hour ;
Sitting attentive at their feet,
They learnt of them a wisdom meet
To strengthen and expand the soul,
And give the intellect control
O'er youthful passions warm, and elevate the whole.

And one from yet a higher source
  Drew wisdom—bending low
At foot of the Redeemer's cross
  Whence streams of Healing flow ;
And we had hoped to see him bear
That Balm of Healing thence—with prayer
Applying it to hearts that bleed ;
To sinners in their hour of need ;
The Great Physician's friend—the preacher of His Creed.

And not far distant from the goal
  Where Jesus holds the prize,
Our younger Aspirant was seen
  With thoughtful—Heaven-set eyes ;

Tho' others passed him in the race,
His was the *firm, unwavering* pace :—
E'en in the Camp's tumultuous bound
The evidence of truth he found,
Sought out with careful zeal in some retired ground.

On the same fiery field they fell—
   The marytrs we have given,
From children of our *hearts* and *homes,*
   To swell the band in Heaven !—
After brief hours of agony
One closed, in hope, his languid eye ;
The other by long days of pain
Made perfect, found in dying—gain ;
Leaving the toils of war for Jesus' peaceful reign.

O would we bring *our martyrs* back
   From *that serene repose ;*
Or pluck the sparkling laurel wreath
   From their heroic brows ?
Oh no ! *we glory* in their fate
Although our hearts are desolate ;
And in our ear, with saddest tone,
One mother makes her piteous moan ;
The other a heart-rending cry
Sends for her first-born to the sky,
While bending 'neath the Cross in prayerful agony !

Come down, Eternal One, and cheer—
   Bring healing on Thy wing
Thou Spirit of the Holy God !
   Till our afflicted sing
A song of triumph in their woe,
Full of thanksgiving, and the flow

Of love divine ;—Shed Heavenly Peace ;
Bid their sad sighs of anguish cease ;
    O make them see
Thy mercy in the stern decree,
That called their darlings hence to homes prepared by
    Thee.
December 3d, 1864.

Lines.

SUGGESTED BY THE EARLY AND LAMENTED DEATH OF C. E.
LEVERETT, JR., THE AUTHOR OF "SUNSHINE."

BELOVED thou hast passed away—
Thy body sleeps in death—thy lay
    No longer thrills us here ;
Sleep sweetly loving heart and true—
And may a stranger pause and strew
Some flowers upon thy grave—and dew
    Their fragrance with a tear ?

Basking in "sunshine" of the Blest,
Thy spirit finds eternal rest
    In Paradise of God—
Breathing the uncorrupted air
Of Eden bowers bright and fair,
And drinking of the fountain clear
    That gushes from her sod.

We would not have thee back again
Where all is sorrow, care and pain;
    Where anguish wrings the soul;
The whole creation groaning lies—
Tears mingle with our sacrifice;
Our earthly "sunshine" quickly hies,
    And Death is in the bowl!

No—let thy spirit, freed from care,
Wing its pure flight along the air
    That waves the Heavenly bowers;
Altho' upon our cheerless way
We miss thy keen wit's lambent play;
Like sword-blade flashing in the ray
    Of "sunshine" bright with showers!

I ever thought "our quarrel just,"
But thou didst deeper plant the trust
    I placed in God and Heaven;
For, if thy spirit, ere it flew
To bathe in clear, celestial dew,
Pronounced our sacred struggle *true*
    I know that Victory's given.

Then banished far be every fear
That darkens now the wintry air,
    And hangs the pall of night
Between us and the coming ray
That yet shall break a glorious day,
All nations leading in the way
    Of happiness and light.

Vanish all visions of the tomb—
The Day-star rises—clears the gloom—
    Redemption has been wrought!
He who has sent His son to die
Has freely promised—"All things I
Will to my faithful ones supply,
    Yea, blessings above thought!"

Then let us take the precious gift,
And grateful homage upward lift
    To the Eternal Word:
See to it that our lives agree
With all His precepts—that we be
A people holy, pure and free
    Whose Ruler is THE LORD.

In Memory of Mrs. Cornelia M. Gregg,

OF COLUMBIA, S. C.,

MOTHER OF GENERAL MAXCY GREGG, WHO DIED SUDDENLY IN AUGUST, 1862, A FEW MONTHS BEFORE HER HEROIC SON.

How beautiful is age when such as thine!
Dear honored friend! just found and lost again,
Before the seed of love could germinate
And spring up in our hearts a perfect flower,
Filling them with its fragrance: *Not before*
It left an impress of perfection there
Never to be effaced. Thy well-stored mind,

Content not with the knowledge it had culled
And garnered up for use, put ever forth
New energy and freshly gathered more,
And from its store dispensed to all around.
The young, delighted, would about thee draw
To hear the pleasant tenor of discourse
Flow from thy ready lips—the while thine eye
Kindled with brightness, and thy warm, kind heart
Shed the true charm o'er all. The middle-aged
Learnt 'twas not time to rest in slothful ease,
With sun just at meridian, but reap on
And gather in their stores for wintry use
And fireside-feasts instructive. While compeers
Joined in the beauty of thy green old age,
And held it forth admiringly to all.

The silent stars keep watch above thy grave,
And thine is rest eternal! But not *there*,
In the cold, clodded earth—above the stars,
Near to the Throne of God, where angels chant
Untiringly their glorious hymn of praise.
No more with anxious thought for *one* afar
Shall throb thy breast maternal—nor thy heart,
O'er-fraught, bow down beneath its weight of love.
All now is joy seraphic—cares of earth,
Lost in the bosom of the Sea of Peace
Shall thence arise no more—while rays of light
Play o'er its waves from the effulgent Sun;—
Gleams of the higher bliss to be revealed.

Jehovah gave and He has ta'en away!
Then let us bow submissive to the blow
Dealt by His own right hand—the Hand of Love!—
For through the blood of the Immaculate

All chastisements are now the signs of love
And tokens of acceptance.   Whom He loves
The Eternal Father chastens for their good;
And the all-pitying heart of Jesus throbs,
On the Great Throne as erst it throbbed on earth.

Let not a stranger hand dare lift the veil
That covers sacred grief—or stranger eye
Peer in too closely.   Rather let them weep
Soft, silent tears; and sympathetic heart,
Aching at core, send fervent, solemn prayer
To the all-merciful and gracious God
For the afflicted.—"Holy Father bless,
Shower Thy love upon them; give them peace
Through the great Comforter, in Christ the Lord."

Maxcy Gregg.

—

Long have I lingered by the lovely mount
  Where our great hero lies,
To hear some gifted bard, in song, recount
  His deeds of high emprise;
Some great historic minstrel sweep the string
  And downward fling
A requiem, telling of a nation's grief,
  Bringing the soul relief—
Or chant of praise to roll for aye along,
  A deathless tide of song,
Spreading and deepening—till our rising youth,
Laved by its sacred wave, reflect his crystal truth!

No sound nor voice was heard,
Save "cherup" of a bird
Sharp-falling on the stillness—or to ear attent
The far off river lent
The pleasant music of its soothing moan
Rushing o'er bed of stone.

All hushed—but now a note
Seems on the breeze to float,
Borne upward from the city—Spreading fair
Beneath the golden air
Of the rich sunset hour;—
No voice of strength or power
But the sweet tribute of a youthful heart
Ready to do his part;
Who, since the great heroic bards are mute,
Strikes, with the hand of love, his garland-dighted lute!*

" 'Twas in the winter wild "
They bore her dauntless child
Back to his mother on his spotless shield,
And laid him to his rest
Within her yearning breast,
Where, like a happy child, he now reposes;—
And as in days of yore,
His morning gambols o'er,
He lay, all flushed and happy from his toy,
And slept, their darling boy!
Between his parents—so in death he lies
'Neath Carolina's skies,
While Spring, her crown of roses
Half shaded in a drapery of woe,
Comes on with footsteps slow

*Lines on the death of General Gregg by a lad of thirteen.
14

To scatter flowers upon the triple mound
            Soft swelling from the ground,
Where *they*, whose love was stronger far than Death,
            Wait the reviving breath
Of that fresh morn when bursting graves shall yield
The precious seed laid up to bloom in Heavenly Field!

            Struck down in noon of life
            Amid the battle strife,
What great eclipse fell then upon the State!
            How dimly broke the morn—
            How sad—whose early dawn
Came ushered in with tidings of *thy fate!*
            Carolina, in her darksome grief,
Bowed low her stately head and sought in tears relief!

            Patriot and statesman true!
         · Long shall thy country rue
The keen-eyed watchman, wont from silent tower,
            With calm prophetic gaze
            To scan the rising haze
That o'er the sunny South began to lower,
Presaging that the hour was nigh
When a terrific storm should sweep across the sky!

            It came with bloody hue—
            Thy sword, the tried and true
Leapt from its scabbard where it long had lain,
            And in thy grasp of might,
            All glowing for the fight,
Streamed like a meteor o'er the gory plain!
Each soldier hailed its cheering ray,
And followed, with a shout, where'er it led the way!
            Quick at his chieftain's call
            He left the Council-Hall,

With statesmen met to save the common weal—
  Ready for any fate,
  So he could check the hate
Of foes vindictive in their deadly zeal,
But not on Carolina's soil
Was he to meet the blow that eased him of his toil!

    'Twas 'neath thy saddened eyes
    He paid *that* sacrifice
Virginia!—but his last fond sigh was given
    To his loved home afar,
    His true soul's polar star!
For her he rendered back his life to Heaven,
And cheerfully his languid eye
Saw through the film of death, her independence nigh!

    A pure immortal fame
    Gilds thy heroic name,
Which soon the polished marble shall record :—
    Thank God we there may write,
    With pencil dipped in light,
"He placed his hope in the Eternal Word;
And on his Saviour's bleeding breast
Laid his war-wearied head in calm and peaceful rest!"
  Columbia, April 14th, 1863.

The Two Last Messages of Maxcy Gregg.

———

COMRADES! our bloody work is done,
The battle fought, the victory won;
Stack arms! and take your well-earned rest,
With thankful prayer to Heaven addressed
　　　For His protecting care.
But pause—new banners flaunt the sky,
The tramp of arméd feet is nigh,
　　　Of subtilty beware!
I must unto the front and know,
What signs yon proud gonfalons show;
Scan if they Federal ensigns be,
Or symbols of our Chivalry!

He said and slightly shook the rein—
His war-steed sped across the plain
With flashing eye, and flowing mane;
No need to wound his glossy side
With prick of rowel—proud was he
To bear the Rose of Chivalry!

Fair Rose! so soon in dust to bide—
Alas! was there no warning cry,
No shout to tell the foe was nigh!
No arm to ward the deadly blow
That laid the warrior-statesman low!
No angel hovering o'er the field
To interpose his guardian shield!—
Withdrawn was God's protecting power
In this the saddest, darkest hour

For Carolina !   Whose great heart
Bled at its inmost core to part
With him, the bravest and the best
Of all her darlings laid to rest:
Her noble champion and knight,
Of 'scutcheon pure and honor bright !

" Quick, surgeon, tell me ' Is it Death ?'
Speak boldly—nor with faltering breath
Try to disguise the truth, for I
Have looked him calmly in the eye
On many a bloody field—nor now,
Though to his mighty power I bow,
Fear his stern glance and haughty brow."

" E'en so :—Submissively I hear
The solemn truth that I am near
The confine of the hidden sphere ;—
But let me ere Death sets his seal
To all my efforts for her weal,
Send the sad message of my fate
To my beloved—my native State;
Tell her—if now I am to die,
I give my life right cheerfully,
And hail her independence nigh."
And with these touching words he threw
His heart's deep love in *that* adieu !

And yet a depth below *that deep*
Must now be fathomed for the love
Which said " Bereaved one do not weep,
But meet me in that home above,
Where dearest we no more shall part
But dwell together ; heart to heart

Beating in concert, at the feet
Of Him, who came my soul to meet
Here, in this wilderness of Death,
And healed it with His pardoning breath."

Columbia, April 21st, 1863.

The Burial of Brig.-General M. Jenkins,

AT SUMMERVILLE, WHIT-SUNDAY, MAY 15TH, 1864.

BRING blossoms from the rosy beds of May,
Bay from the woodland, Myrtle from the bowers,
And arbor-vitæ, whose enduring leaf
Symbols the life eterne; and let fair hands
Weave them in garlands to adorn the mound
Where sleeps the brave and true. Sweet his repose
Near the maternal bosom from whose fount
He drew the virtues that made up his life.
A few short weeks ago that silent breast
Throbbed with a holy joy, when to her heart
The mother pressed her young, heroic son
And bade him, with her blessing, go again
And battle for his country. Long then seemed
Their day of meeting—but God made it short.

Here is no martial note, nor organ's swell
To honor, with its wild or solemn strain
Our hero's burial—but one lone bird
Pours on the fragrant air a shower of song.

Sing on sweet warbler! for what holier note
Can charm him to his rest, than thine Heaven-taught
And flowing, like the angels' from a breast,
Wholly at peace with God! Heart-soothing strain!
How different from the noisy din of strife,
The war-trump and the cannon's awful roar—
Glide softly to the mourners sorrowing hearts
And fit them for the promise of *this day*,
The Comforter sent forth to all who weep,
And bearing dews of healing on His wing!

One blessed Sabbath, when the Lenten Fast
Was drawing to its close, and streaks of light,
As heralding the glorious Easter morn,
Began to pierce the gloom, we saw thee bow
Within this Temple, and on bended knee
Receive in reverent hand the bread divine,
And carry to thy lips the wine of Life,
Which to the heart of faith is Heavenly food,
We little deemed it thy viaticum—
And that by Whitsuntide thy mortal frame
Would have been given to the silent dust,
With tears of kindred—and a Nation's grief!

We thought to see thee, in the coming time,
When meek-eyed Peace has once more blessed our land—
Wearing the laurel-wreath thy valor won,
And clothed in garments of prosperity,
Living to good old age, with "troops of friends"
And children's children gathered 'round thy hearth,
Thy warm, bright Southern hearth—to hear thee tell
Of deeds of prowess by our heroes wrought
In the great struggle—but with modest grace
Setting aside thine own—We fondly dreamed—
But God has willed it otherwise—Farewell!

True soldier of thy Country and of Christ!
With what assured hope we leave thee here
To wait th' Archangel's trump! Thy spirit fled
Upon the shout of triumph—and the sound
Took a seraphic sweetness as thy soul,
Nearing the gate of Paradise, was met
By throng of white-robed spirits bearing palms,
And singing hymns of Victory and Peace!

A Wild-Flower Wreath,

FOR THE GRAVE OF SARAH E. WISE.

My last green chaplet graced a hero's grave! *
A martyr to the sacred cause of Truth—
Whose soul from front of battle leaped to God,
And now reposes near the Saviour's Throne.

That garland scarce has withered, when again
I gather flowerets for another mound,
And as my trembling fingers twine the wreath
Do keep them fresh and dewy with my tears.

Martyr as well was she whom now we weep,
The silent sufferer, who so bravely bore
Sad exile from her noble, bleeding State;
Who bowed her tender shoulders to the cross
With maiden meekness, and submissive faith,
Having no other will save Christ the Lord's,
Who placed it there, and bade her follow Him.

* Brigadier-General Jenkins.

Weep not for her—for surely from *that cross*,
Of anguish and unrest, her soul has been
Borne up by angels to reposing bowers
Fast by the gate of Heaven where the redeemed
Await, in blissful hope, the Judgment morn.

But for the stricken-one—The Mother forced †
To part with the sole treasure left to cheer
The lonesome hours of exile, care and toil,
And lighten all life's burdens, let us weep,
Mingling warm drops of sympathy with her's—
O what a void in that large, loving heart!
But God can fill it—and we know He will,
For tenderest pity swells the pleading breast
Of the God-man before His Father's Throne,
And what He asks the Spirit will perform.

Come then and whisper of His boundless love
Ye friends who minister to this distress,
And let your words of comfort fall as dew
From heart of Heaven upon the tender plants.

Tell how her dear-one dwells where angels love
To tend on precious souls redeemed by Christ,
And brought to realms of Bliss; and, wandering, catch
Slight glimpses of the mystery their eyes
Have vainly sought to pierce, tho' formed of rays
Effulgent from the fountain-head of Light!

Tell how her intellect, so brilliant here,
Shall there expand, until a glorious orb,

---

† Mrs. Margaret Wise, of Virginia, sister of the Ex-Governor of that State.

15

Of perfect and harmonious symmetry,
It floats towards the Wisdom ‡ that was found
Linked to the throne of God ere Time began.

Tell how His pity spared her gallant sons
When battling for their country—not cut off
In heat of conflict, without time to cry
"God save my spirit"—or, "Have mercy Christ"—
But given yet a longer day of grace
To make their peace with God—if haply they
Have not already found it in His Son.

O give us all *that peace*—Thou Blessed One!
Not only to this sorrow-stricken soul—
But unto all who mourn throughout the length
And breadth of our distracted, bleeding land—
Let it distill as dew upon our heads,
And in our hearts be amply shed abroad
Leaving no room for harrowing doubt or fear.

Then, should our eyelids close before the day
When the glad messenger of Hope is seen
Winging its way with olive-branch of Peace
To plant in our rich soil, we will not grieve,
But—leaving our offspring to enjoy its shade,
And feast upon its fruitage—speed away
To find its glorious prototype—in Heaven.

  Columbia, July 16th, 1864.

---

   ‡ See eighth chapter of Proverbs.

War-Waves.

A CHANT FOR THE TIMES.

WHAT are the war-waves saying
  As they compass us around?
The dark, ensanguined billows,
  With their deep and dirge-like sound?
Do they murmur of submission;
  Do they call on us to bow
Our necks to the foe triumphant
  Who is riding o'er us now?—

Never!—No sound submissive
  Comes from those waves sublime,
Or the low, mysterious voices
  Attuned to their solemn chime!
For the hearts of our noble martyrs
  Are the springs of its rich supply;
And those deeply mystic murmurs
  Echo their dying cry!

They bid us uplift our banner
  Once more in the name of God;
And press to the goal of Freedom
  By the paths our fathers trod:
They passed o'er their dying brothers,
  From their pale lips caught the *sigh*—
The *flame* of their hearts heroic
  From the flash of each closing eye!

Up! up! for the time is pressing,
  The red waves close around;—
They will lift us on their billows
  If our hearts are faithful found!

They will lift us high—exultant
　And the craven world shall see
The Ark of a ransomed people
　Afloat on the crimson sea!

Afloat—with her glorious banner—
　The cross on its field of red,
Its stars, and its white folds waving
　In triumph at her head:—
Emblem of all that's sacred
　Heralding Faith to view;—
Type of unblemished Honor;
　Symbol of all that's true!

Then what can those waves be singing
　But an anthem, grand, sublime,
As they bear for our martyred heroes
　A wail to the verge of Time?
What else as they roll majestic
　To the far off shadowy shore,
To join the Eternal chorus
　When time shall be no more?

Columbia, December 19th, 1863.

Columbia.

SAD exiles from our lowland nest,
Could we have found a sweeter rest,
Than on thy fair and fragrant breast
　　　　　　　Columbia?

Sheltered in thy caressing arms,
We scarcely heed the wild alarms
Of war—so potent are thy charms
　　　　　　　Columbia!

Yet sometimes, startled from our trance
We cast around a troubled glance
At tidings of the foe's advance
     Columbia.

As lately when *my city* fair
Bristled with carabine and spear:
Her forts with triumph hailed them near,
     Columbia!

Then valiant Beauregard and Rhett,
New jewels in their helmets set;
And gallant Ripley cried "well met"
     Columbia!

Secure again we turn to thee
Decked in the Spring's sweet witchery,
And 'mid the buds keep jubilee
     Columbia.

How can the heart be sad when here
The sunlight glances everywhere;
And song-birds vocal make the air,
     Columbia!

Thy lovely avenues invite,
Now with the fresh green foliage dight,
To wander on in glad delight
     Columbia.

Thy Park! that fairy-like retreat
So often pressed by maiden feet,
When in coquettish sport they meet,
     Columbia.

And when 'neath Summer's sunset sky
Thy precious "wee-ones" thither hie,
What holier scene can greet the eye,
Columbia!

Thy gardens! not closed up in pride,
And to the Refugee denied—
But gates thrown courteously wide,
Columbia.

Where, for the fragment of an hour,
We deem us in some magic bower,
And flit entranced from flower to flower,
Columbia!

Thy churches! where the exile's care
Is lulled by solemn hymn and prayer;
And the *sure trust* that God is near,
Columbia.

O beautiful!   O fair to see!
Spreading o'er sunny slope and lea:
Embraced by rich-voiced Congaree,
Columbia!

Where the stern mountain virtues meet
The lowland graces, soft and sweet;
And form a character complete,
Columbia!

Long shall the exile's blessing rest
Upon thy warm and loving breast;
Thy noble, honorable crest,
Columbia!

April 16th, 1863.

Note.—Columbia presents a different aspect since the visit of the great raider, Sherman.

To My Sister,

ON VISITING HER NEW HOME, MAY, 1864.

" PEACE to this house and all who dwell herein "—
Peace—and the benediction of thy God
Rest on thy homestead sister! The soft wing
Of the Eternal Spirit shelter give ;
And the Good Shepherd guard it as His fold.

The period of thy married life has been
A cycle rich in blessings—for altho'
The clouds that oft' times shadow wedded bliss
Could not be kept forever from thy sky,
Yet have they always proved but summer rack
Which the sweet breath of peace soon drove afar,
Leaving free scope for the warm Sun of Love.

At times the chill of poverty has crept
Almost too near thy heart, when at thy door
The form of cold-eyed Penury was seen
About to lift the latch ; but the strong arm,
And firm determination of the one,
Given by Heaven, to be thy Lord and Head,
Held him at bay, while with unwavering faith
He labored on to keep his babes from want ;
And now, at length, with grateful heart he sees
His faith rewarded and his labor blessed.

During those many years the Hand of God
Added, from time to time, a precious flower
Unto the wreath of beauty twining round
Thy homestead, and the altar of thy heart.

O marvellous, unprecedented Love!—
In all this score of years no flower or bud
Has fallen from the garland to the dust!
The six bay blossoms and four roses still
Shed their perfume and gladden thy new home.

But O, my sister! it were vain to hope,
If God should spare thy life a few more years,
(Which may He do, for love of His dear Son,
And tender pity to thy little ones,)
Thou canst escape for aye the cruel pang
That wrings the heart maternal when it feels
A lovely floweret drooping its fair head
And bowing pale in death.   It cannot be
But that the sword must pierce thy bosom too
E'en as the Holy Mary's.   Then, Beloved,
With humble, penitential, prayerful soul
Prepare thee for the trial—tho' it be
One of thy hero boys to offer up
In sacrifice upon thy country's shrine,
Or see thy little precious rosy pet
Removed from *thine* to bloom on JESUS' breast.

Would that a sister's love could ward the blow!—
Most gladly would I suffer cruel pain
To save thy heart one pang.   It cannot be—
The mandate has gone forth we all must die;
Yet have I heard the Christian mother's breast,
Feels a mysterious pleasure in its pain,
When she can say, " I have a flower with God "—
A lamb of mine within the Saviour's Fold!

Then let me with a calm, confiding trust
Commend thee to our tender Father's care,
He loves thee with a love surpassing mine;

And when He chastens mercy guides the blow.
O may the whirlwind fury of His wrath
Never sweep o'er this dwelling, but its change
Come on with noiseless tread ; till " calm decay,"
With ivyed beauty, makes its walls sublime;
And as we reckon those who, one by one,
Shall from its portal pass to worlds unknown,
May we, with strong assurance, feel that they,
With garments lily-white, have entrance found
To the Eternal Mansions of The Blest.

The New.

" O'CONNOR'S CHILD."

Dedicated to the infant Mary Louisa O'Connor, aged 4 months.

O'Connor's Child!   Tho' not "the bud
Of Erin's Royal tree of glory,"
Yet hast thou graces of thine own
To live in song or story—
Thy winsome mouth—thine eyes of light
So wildly, beautifully bright
And blue withal—thy gestures free,
And eloquent of baby glee,
All seem prophetic of a power
To be revealed in Love's own hour,
When bards about thy path shall throng
To offer thee the need of song.

In sooth thou art " a hero's child "—
For in the front of battle wild,
Thy sire has often bravely stood
When Death was sweeping, as a flood,
His comrades from his side ; and who—
When Victory turned the tide of war
On dread Manassas' plain—but he
Planted the Legion Banner bright,
Upon the captured battery's height,
And with exultant gesture threw
Its folds unto the breeze—that far
Bore his triumphant, glad " hurrah "—
While war-worn comrades joined the cry,
And swelled, with grateful hearts, the shout of Victory !

Fair, lovely child !   When o'er thy head
Three fleeting lustres shall have shed
The influence of their suns and showers ;—
And culture rare, in fireside hours
Of chilly winter, shall have wrought
On thy young mind, and from it brought
The fruit and flowerage of thought
To crown thy spring-time : Then shall we
None brighter 'mong the maidens see ;
None more bewitching—with the grace
Of Erin in thy form and face ;
Her fire within thine eye—thy hair
Bound with her shamrock green and fair ;
While round her Harp thy dimpled arms shall twine,
And rosy fingers 'wake a music half divine !

Child of the ancient Holy Isle !—
May the Eternal Father's smile
Beam ever on thee !   His fond eye

Watch o'er thy heedless infancy ;
His guardian arm, through life, embrace
And bear thee on from Grace to Grace,
Till thou perfected stand before His sacred face!

Columbia, December 17, 1863.

Lizzie.

BEAUTIFUL and bright and airy
Is our youthful friend !   A fairy
Must have blessed her natal morn,
With each grace that can adorn
Circle gay, or homestead holy :—
Round her golden locks a glory
Gleams, as from a maiden saint,
Free from every earthly taint,
That from old Cathedral aisle
Greets us with a placid smile.

Then anon her bright eye glances
Beam that every heart entrances,
Telling that sweet love reposes
Like perfume in heart of roses,
Deep within her gentle breast,
Tho' to mortal ne'er confest!

Witching creature !   Soft, caressing,
Shedding o'er thy home a blessing
Such as seldom doth endower
Mortal dwelling.   Lovely flower !

To thy sister flowerets showing
All the sacred graces flowing
From a life devote *to duty ;*
In itself the greatest beauty
Can adorn a maiden—Grace
Adding to the fairest face.

Brothers, mindful of the glory
Of their name renowned in story,
Lay their laurels at *thy feet,*
Thou who makes their dwelling meet
For the weary soldiers' rest—
Pillowed on thy gentle breast
They forget past toil and care ;
While thine ever ready ear
Drinks in with a proud delight
Incidents of Camp or Fight.

Heart paternal, ever blessing
Doth the hand of love caressing
Pass o'er every rippling curl
Of thy hair, thou fairy girl!
Deeming thee the sweetest flower
Of his garland-dighted bower ;
Minding of Love's early day
When a richer treasure lay
On his breast—in joy or care
Shedding blessed fragrance *there.*

But there is a grace supernal
From the Cross of the Eternal
Son of God forever streaming—
Is its glory o'er thee beaming ?
Is thy beauteous robe and vestal

Fastened by the pearl Celestial,
O'er thy breast of snowy whiteness?—
Jewel above price and brightness,
By the Bridegroom only given
Holy souls elect of Heaven.
Is it thine?—If so, no sorrow
Dims the brightness of thy morrow;
Or, should clouds arise with day,
God shall chase them swift away,
And a light ethereal pour
O'er thy pathway—evermore!

Eliza.

TINY lock of baby hair!
Brings a vision sweet and fair
To my fancy's ken to-day;
Rural cottage far away,
Canopied by sighing pines—
Trellised by protecting vines,
That encircle it around
Like arm of rustic lover wound
About the dear-one he would shield
From danger of the wood or field.

In the porch a hammock swings—
To its side the baby clings,
Thumping, jumping, laughing, crowing,
All unconscious she is throwing
Gladness over hearts deprest,
Weary of the stern unrest
Of this arid wilderness!—

"Who are these whom thus to bless
God has sent this precious dove,
In the fulness of His love
From the Mercy Seat above?"

These through fiery scenes have past!—
By the war's terrific blast
Driven to this sheltering bower,
They await, in faith, the hour
When a word from God's own mouth
Shall call back blessings on The South!

Grandam—once with graceful mien
And matron dignity, as queen
Reigned she over acres fair;
Loved, respected far and near;
Guiding with religious hand
Children dear and menial band,
Ever ready at command;—
Still her children to her cling;
But her servants, on swift wing
Of false freedom, all have flown,
Leaving, in old age, alone
One who had been ever kind,
Serving *them* with hand and mind,
Since when a bride of sixteen years
She came with blushes and with tears,
A Southern planter's life to share,
Its joys, its comfort and its care;
Till now, when on her widowed head,
Three score and ten long years have shed
The snows of winter—*They* have gone!
But the Good God leaves not alone,
And void of comfort, one whose days

Have been devoted to His praise—
For, yet enough of strength has she
To ply her needle busily—
At the attic window seated
While her listening ear is greeted
With melodious strains that flow
From violin and piano—
Linked harmoniously below!
Or, for a while, her task she leaves
To snatch her namesake from the bed,
(With her impromptu toys o'erspread)
To see the silvery rain-drops fall,
And point her rosy finger small
At the bright globules as they float
To patter in the mimic.moat
Formed by the dripping from the eaves!

Father—prematurely grey—
From paternal fields away,
Where his serfs usurp the sway
God committed to his hand:—
Four brave sons around him stand,
With loving heart and baréd breast,
Ready to do his least behest.
The arms that struck for Liberty
Will link around the old roof tree
And prop it for futurity!—

But in these dark and gloomy days
Eliza! all your pretty ways
Have formed his chief delight—You shine
His "Iris" beautiful, divine;
Traced by Light's pencil rich and warm,
His bow of promise in the storm!

To your *Mother's* breast you bring
The olive-branch of peace, and sing
A song of Hope within her ear
So penetrating, soft and clear
It floats adown through many a year!

"Cousin mine, you have not told
Half the joy that I unfold;
My *dear brothers* from the fight
Make it now their chief delight
To toss the baby to and fro;
Quick from arm to arm I go—
Mirth dispensing, Gloom preventing
As they toss me to and fro!—
Even *Cousin John* you see
Leaves his book to romp with me!
I will be as proud I ween
As any little Fairy Queen
Sporting on the moonlit 'knowe,'
While Elf-boys around her bow!"

Cease!—and let dear Cousin Kate
Limerick's crownéd Laureate
Your wonder-working power relate:—
When the fretful hour draws nigh,
And little babe should close her eye
For her health-preserving rest,
She *will not* sleep on mother's breast!
"At morning, noon, or dewy eve"
Cousin Theus her work must leave
To lull the darling to repose;
No plaintive lullaby she throws,
Full of pathetic charm to close

Those heavy lids—but babe *must* go
    Whether she would or know,
To sleep—for coz *will* have it so!
    With thump and bump
    And noise and clatter
(Without giving "miss" a voice in the matter)
    Enough to fright
    The little sprite,
    Yclepéd slumber,
    And the number
Of moth-like elves that round her cling,
Bearing dreams upon their wing;
    But no such thing,
Babe is lapped by Slumber's wing!

See, the sunset golden shafts
Shoot across the road! and laughs
The breeze amid the boughs—Opprest!
Come and take an hour of rest,
And quaff the aromatic air,
Bidding short farewell to care:
Babe the pure delight must share;
AUNT will wheel her Car of State—
(In which she's sitting proud, elate—
Waiting by the step or gate)
Through the long symphonious reaches
Of the pines, whose whisper teaches
Of the Land of deep repose:
What sweet music earthward flows!
As if Good Spirits in their flight *
Heavenward, had, in mid air,

---

* The idea of the pausing of the spirits in their heavenward flight,
borrowed from my friend, Dr. J. B. Irving.

16

Paused to give us mortals cheer,
Striking from harmonious wing
Echoes, soft as those which ring
The Beatific Bowers of Light
Spread below the Eternal Height!

Lamplight flashes in the hall!
With her shadow on the wall
Babe will play till " Good-night all "—
Laughing, crowing, clawing, toying;
In her very heart enjoying
This her first essay to clasp
A shadow that eludes her grasp!

Cottage 'neath the waving pines;
Claspéd by the graceful vines!
Oft, by love-lit fancy borne,
I visit thee at night and morn,
Enter at window or at door
To romp with baby on the floor;
Or take new lessons to my soul
Of Christian graces to control
Its restless throbbings—here they shine
In tints so tender, so divine—
So beautifully glow to view
They needs must prove Religion true;
Only the Gospel's blessed ray
Could give such light in this dark day!

FATHER! where'er my dear ones roam
May Christ's religion make their dome
Radiant with Faith, and Hope, and Love
Until they rest with Thee above
In mansions whence is no re-move!

October, 1865.

Little Harriet's Dream.

O what a beautiful dream I had last night! I dreamt I was in heaven, and saw the bright angels all holding hands in a ring, and singing praise to God. And I thought one of the angels, dressed in shining gold, took me by the hand and said, "Come and sing with us," but I said, "I cannot *rest* till Jesus and brother Charley come."

Then I looked up and saw Jesus, leading brother Charley by the hand, coming to us. Brother was dressed in his soldier clothes, and had his cap on his head. He looked just as when I told him "good-by."

Jesus was a soldier too—but had no cap upon His head. He took me by the hand and led me to the angels, and we all began to sing. Jesus was singing too!

I saw God sitting upon His shining throne. The throne was made of white pearls and black diamonds. And God was as bright and shining as when He talked with Moses in The Mount.

But I was not afraid—I spoke to God and said, "Will you give me some of that white manna you fed the children of Israel with in the wilderness?"

The dream of a child six years old, given in her own words. We were expecting the body of her beloved brother home for burial; and her little heart was full of him.

I DREAMED I stood in heaven
  'Mid a fair and shining throng
Of angels, who sung praise to God
  In sweet and solemn song;
And as they sang they linked their hands
  And formed a circle bright,
Moving harmoniously around
  All robed in dazzling white.

On seeing me one broke the ring
　And took me by the hand,
Saying "Come darling up with me
　And join the shining band;"
I said "I cannot *rest* e'en here,
　In *this* my promised Home,
Until the Saviour, whom I love,
　And brother Charley come!"

Then up I lifted face and eye,
　And lo! the Saviour dear,
Leading my brother by the hand,
　With beaming smile drew near:
I knew my Brother, ah! so well,
　He wore Confederate grey—
Dressed as a soldier was our boy,
　Just as he went away!

He had his cap upon his head,
　Drawn low to shade his eye,
Just as he looked when last I saw
　And bade him *then* "Good-by"—
Blest Jesus shone a soldier too,
　With sword upon His thigh,
As "Captain of Salvation"—he
　With conquering step drew nigh!

He wore no helmet on His head,
　But His rich, golden hair
Swept o'er His mailéd shoulders broad,
　In ripples soft and fair;
His girdle studded was with gems,
　All glorious to behold,
His feet like burnished metal shone,
　Fine brass, or finer gold!

He kindly took me by the hand
   And led me to the ring,
Where Christ, and brother Charles and I
   Did with the angels sing!
For so it seeméd in my dream—
   O was it *very wrong*,
To think that Jesus lent His voice
   To swell the angels' song?

And then I thought I saw the King
   Of Glory on his Throne;
The great, the everlasting God,
   The bright and shining One:
The Throne was made of creamy pearls
   And diamonds black as jet,
The lustre of the *one* against
   The *other* meetly set.

And in my dream I spoke to God
   The Father, tho' He shone,
As when he talked upon the Mount
   To Moses all alone!
And said " My FATHER will you feed
   Me with that manna white,
With which you fed, when in The Wild,
   The wandering Israelite?"

" Not that, I give thee better bread,"
   A loving voice replied,
" For thou shalt feed upon the Lamb
   Of God, who meekly died :—
My Christian Children all must live
   Upon the food divine,
The flesh and blood of Jesus Christ
   Set forth in bread and wine."

With this I 'woke, and wept to find
   That I was lingering here,
Till reaching out my little hand
   I touched my Mother dear;
Then was I glad to think' that I
   Might still her comfort prove,
Until we join our darling *there*,
   Where all is peace and Love!
November 28, 1865.

An Echo from Summerville.

DEDICATED TO THE "LADIES' MEMORIAL ASSOCIATION" OF
CHARLESTON, SO. CA.

EXQUISITE music floateth free
From "the old City by the Sea,"
   Half jubilant, half drear,
It fills mine eyes with holy tears;
Recalls the hope of former years,
The mingled faith and love:—The fears
Would some time loom upon the scene,
   Clothing the sky serene
   In clouds that came between
   Us, and the rainbow hues,
   All gloriously diffused,
   Begot of sunny ray
   Upon the crystal spray
Spanning, with arc of light, the visionary sphere.

The breeze seems full of sighs;
And low pathetic cries,
As from the snowy breast
Of woman when opprest
   With grief profound—
Yet list!—another sound!
A song of triumph mingling with the moan,
   And all around are thrown
Strains, as from viewless spirits blending low,
Sweet music with the notes that from those mourners
   flow!

It is the chosen day,
When women homage pay,
To those have perished in a cause as high
   As ever lit the eye
Or stirred the spirit of heroic knight!
   None other can compare,
   Save *that* which in yon sphere
Places the crown of Christian martyrhood
Upon the foreheads of the brave and good,
   A garland dazzling bright,
   Wove of celestial light!

They come—the bright and fair!
With hearts true to the cause,
The holy, patriot laws
Of God and man, to strew with flower-buds rare
   The graves where calmly sleep
   The forms that erst did sweep
   Across the gory plain,
   Carrying, within their train,
Death and destruction to the haughty foe;

Till God's mysterious power,
In one o'erwhelming hour
O'erthrew their hopes, and laid their banners low
With stern, chastising blow !

Come on and pour the dirge—
We stand upon the verge
Of utter ruin.   All in vain! in vain !
The ghastly wounds, the blood that fell as rain
Upon the war-bruised Earth—the dying groan
Of sire, son and brother,
And the mate
Of heart left desolate :—
One dies on battle-field; the while another
In gloomy prison ward would gladly smother
The sigh of anguish piercing to the soul
Of bleeding comrade dear,
Whose life is ebbing there;
The stern control
Causes the beaded sweat adown his face to roll !

In vain ?—Say not "in vain"—
Dispel the dismal strain,
And feed the summer air with anthems high !
The God who fills the sky,
And walketh on the whirlwind, still is near,
And bends a listening ear—
His Holy Eye,
Will not behold, unchecked, iniquity !
The sands run on apace
And bring the Day of Grace,
When once more, hand in hand,
We shall unshackled stand
And breathe the breath of Freemen in the State,
Where God has fixed our fate !

Then catch we up the music as it floats,
    And add exultant notes
As we pass on to lay our garlands fair,
    Beaded with Memory's tear,
      Upon the *three* loved graves *
      O'er which bright Nature waves
Her coronal of ever changing hues;
      Where Evening sheds her dews;
      And holy stars diffuse
The hope that other eyes than ours watch o'er
The heroes whose repose is sacred evermore!
June 16, 1866.

The Southern Boy's Lament.

WHERE has my dear old maumer gone?
I miss her when the day is done;
I miss her when the rosy ray
Of morn upon my curtains play;
Miss her kind face, her loving eyes,
Her cheery greeting—"Sonny, rise!
The lambs are frisking on the lawn;
The ducklings to the pond have gone;
The hungry chickens 'peep' and cry;
Sweet little Sis has oped her eye;

---

* The graves of Brigadier-General M. E. Jenkins and privates
Henry M. Hughes and Charles B. Foster, who alone of the Confederate dead are interred in Summerville. They rest in the Epis-
copal churchyard.
   17

She has been washed and dressed with care,
And waits for thee—The precious dear!
Up! up! and join her in her play;
And bless God for another day."

Where is my dear old maumer—where?
At night I used to say my prayer
Down at her knee, if mother dear
Was busy—or upon her breast
Held darling sister hushed to rest;
And then, dear maumer, *me* would tell
Of Heaven, where the angels dwell;
Or how the All-Loving Father's eye
Looks down upon us as we lie
Snug in our beds :—of Jesus who
Sits with a crown upon His brow
At God's right hand; *tell* when on Earth
He never silenced childrens' mirth,
Nor frowned the prattlers away ;
But, with a smile as bright as day,
Would woo them to His side and bless
And gather in His arms with loving, warm caress!

When angels brought my pretty sis,
She was the first to let me kiss,
And touch her tender hand and cheek;
She told me that I must be meek,
And kind and loving to the child,
If I would have the Saviour mild
To reckon me His lambkin dear,
One of His own true fold and care.

With maumer's grandson I would play
And romp about the live-long day,

Drilling him, with the other boys,
With roll of drum and trumpet noise;
We fished together at the brook,
A bent pin serving us for hook;
Set traps the pretty birds to catch,
And played at many a merry match:
Where have my happy playmates gone?
I cannot find a single one!
But most of all, my maumer dear,
I cannot find *her* anywhere!

She was not here on Christmas Day
To see the beautiful display
Of treasures brought me by "St. Nick;"
Say mother, is dear maumer sick?—
She was not here to praise each toy,
With eyes brimful of Christmas joy;
Not hear to get my hearty kiss,
Her "Merry Christmas" too I miss;
Not here to join "the angels' song:"—
I missed her *so* the whole day long,—
See here the handkerchief I bought,
With pretty colors richly fraught,
To form a turban for her head—
Oh! tell me mother, is she dead?
Say, will she *never* come again?—
It fills my heart with cruel pain;
And little sister too will cry
If maumer ne'er again shall sing her "hush-a-by."

My boy! Old maumer 's of the past—
On her dear face we've looked our last;
No more o'er our sick beds shall see
Her dark face bending tenderly;

No more she'll fold you in her arms,
Or quiet sister's soft alarms;—
No more will she be by to hail
The new-born infant's feeble wail;
No more with loving, pious care,
Shall robe our darlings for the bier;
Or close the venerable eyes
Of pilgrim ready for the skies :
Nor weep at burial of our dead;—
Nor help to deck the marriage bed
Of our young daughters;—nor increase the mirth
When to the old paternal hearth
The boy she proudly nursed upon her breast
Brings his fair bride for aye to rest
A daughter of the house;—Oh! nevermore,
Her heart shall thrill with joys of yore,
While our own bosoms gave responsive swell
Of love, which only GOD'S OMNICIENT WORD can tell.

PART THE THIRD.

Poems, Rural and Miscellaneous.

Needs no show of mountain hoary,
  Winding shore or deepening glen,
Where the landscape in its glory
  Teaches truth to wandering men :
Give true hearts but earth and sky,
And some flowers to bloom and die,
Homely scenes and simple views
Lowly thoughts may best infuse.

                    [KEBLE.

The Flower-Laden Cupid.

The God of Love, *A ! Benedicité,*
How mighty and how grete a Lord is he !
Again his might their gainen non obstacles,
He may be clessed a God for his miracles.
For he can maken at his owen gise
Of everich herte, as that him list devise.

[CHAUCER.

"Cupid lovely ! Cupid bright !
With thine eyes of roguish light ;
Where hast thou been wandering, boy ?
Thou art beaming o'er with joy,
Showing that some mischief gay
Has been wrought along the way ;—
By thy quiver full of flowers,
Thou hast been in Beauty's bowers
Sporting all this blessed day
Of the fragrant, rosy May ;
Thy beatitude reveal—
That its joyance might me steal
From the carking care of earth,—
Cupid fill me with thy mirth ! "

"Jove on me bestowed the power
To sun myself in Beauty's bower ;—
When from my ærial flight
In her shady haunts I light,
Beaming glorious to the sight ;
Lily hands are clapped in glee
And Cupid ' Iö Triumphe !'

Shouted—Then beneath my wing
I hide my bow, and hear them sing—
Yet place the arrow to the string!—
Look among my flowers—see
Not a shaft is left to me!
I have scattered them around,
And with these spoils my quiver crowned.—
Whitest bosoms now are grieving;
Bosoms late with wild bliss heaving;
Eyes that into eyes as bright
Deeply gazed in tranced delight,
Now are weeping, and despair
Fills the once enchanted sphere!

"'Tis a common joy I wis
Thus to sport with maiden bliss—
I, to thee, would gladly tell,
But for laughing, what befell
As I bore my burden light
Venus' Fane to deck at night;—
Right along the roadside lay,
Screenéd from the sun of May
By a vine-entangled bower,
Fairer youth than ever flower
Culled to place on Beauty's breast,
Where he fain himself would rest!
Had my mother seen him there
She had sworn him twice as fair
As Adonis, once so dear:—
Streaked with light, his dark brown hair
Waved around as fine a brow
As ever Phidias carved, I vow;—
His bright eyes outshone the stars—
E'en the golden shafts of Mars,

And the God whose silver beams
Mingle with our morning dreams!—
Easy was his attitude—
No obtruding point or rude
Marred the undulating line,
Of his graceful form's recline :—
Now, methought, for glorious fun
Ere Apollo's car has run
To the western gate of Heaven,
Where he baits his steeds at even.
Soon I reached him—veiling nigh—
With the leaves that 'round my head
Gracefully their drapery spread,—
Half my visage—and an eye,
Lest he should their cunning spy!
Trippingly I went along
Like an infant drunk with song;
Chanting at the top of joy,
"Love met once an idle boy,"
Waking all the echoes gay
With my stirring roundelay!
Vain it fell upon the child
Resting in the forest wild!
As I neared his couch I slipped,
And my quiver downward tipped,
Scattering along the road
All my bright and fragrant load.
In a voice forlorn and drear,
Mimicking a great despair,
I addressed the youth and said :
'Gentle stranger lend thine aid,
I have from my mother strayed;
Help me to regain her treasure
Or she'll chastise without measure,

Me, her poor afflicted son,
For the mischief I have done.' "

" Cupid, think not to beguile,
Said the youth, with scornful smile,
Me with thy deceitful wile,—
Well I know thee—and those flowers,
Saw thee steal from rosy bowers
When the morn was blushing new,
And a light breeze shook the dew
From the leaves and plants—and threw
Perfume forth to hail the day
By Aurora led that way :—
When at noon I passéd by
Naught was heard but wail and sigh,
Rifled maidens' dreary cry—
They were pure and bright at morn
Ere thy warm kiss had withdrawn
All the sweets—but left the thorn!—
I'll not touch the dangerous bloom,
Nor inhale the rich perfume
Of thy blossoms—Yes, I swear
To thine Altar offering ne'er
Of enwreathéd buds to bear;
In Idalian temple high
Never heave a love-lorn sigh."

"By great Aphrodite's power!
By the Gods! thou'lt rue this hour!
Thou shalt bow thy haughty head
Ere another day has sped."

"Tho' my arrows all were spent
Yet a rose-shaft to me lent

Weapon keen enough to kill
Sent by *my* unerring skill!
Shyly I upon the bow
Placed the thorn'd rose—and lo!
On his bosom fell a woe;—
As he felt the keen unrest
Of the thorn within his breast,
Off he started with the bound
Of a wounded stag, with hound
Closely in pursuit—and made
For the thickest sylvan shade;
Trembling all with fear and pain,
Dreaming there he would remain
Till peace and strength returned again!
There a rosy girl he'll meet,
And with love's soft accents greet,
Lowly sighing at her feet!
She will catch his bosom's pain,
And for ease my mother's Fane,
Hand in hand they'll seek to gain—
Then for Love's all glorious reign!"

Lo! the reason of my chant,
Happy, mirthful, jubilant!
Come and join th' exultant glee—
"Cupid—Iö Triumphe!"

A Twilight Walk.

It is the hour when we were wont to rove,
My youthful friend and I.   He is not here,
Yet will I venture forth alone, alone,
And on the bank, where we so oft reclined,
To watch the river in its noiseless flow,
Sit musingly, and twine ideal wreaths,
From Memory's garden culled—that fairy realm—
To deck his thoughtful brow ; flowers brighter far
Than those the rosy-fingered Spring entwines
Around the forest trees, or wakes to life
Beneath the dewy pressure of her feet.
As she comes bounding through the fragrant glade,
Made vocal with the song of happy birds,
Darting in mirth around their bridal bowers,
The flowers of Hope, Love, Joy and holy Peace,
That Heaven-descended bud that blossomed erst
In Paradise beside the Fount of Life—
Lo ! where the golden gates of Heaven unclose,
And gorgeous banners flaunt the evening air,
To welcome the Day-god, with hot haste speeding
Unto his couch of rest !   The western sky
Is all ablaze with crimson, green and gold ;
Whilst cloudy mountains lift their purple heads,
In pomp magnifical, on either side !

How in a moment is the pageant changed !
E'en thus the beauteous visions of our youth
Fade to the dun of manhood ; soon to be
Lost in the night-like darkness of the grave.

The solemn vesper hour now veils the earth
With her dim, fleecy light; her spirit sits
Composedly in yon pale evening star
Upon the border of the sable clouds.

It is the hour when, arm in arm, we turned
Our lingering footsteps homeward—vesper calm
Resting upon our souls, by converse sweet
Engendered; or, the solemn word of Bard
Poured forth in liquid music with the tones
Of thy sweet voice, my Friend. Ah! when shall I
Ever again such happy moments know?
When have a youthful heart repose on mine
With love and trust so perfect? Kindling there,
By his sweet smile, and eyes of dovelike sheen,
And most poetic heart, and Christian soul,
The fire of life—almost burnt out and gone.

And some do smile and think it "passing strange"
That I do love thee with so deep a love,
When thou art but a youth on Being's shore,
And I far launched upon the wave of life.
Unhappy souls! they little ween the joy
Of hearts congenial intertwined in love;
Like clings to like—and souls of kindred stamp
Will mingle—let the cold-eyed sceptic sneer—
Though one be lodged in form of palsied eld,
The other in a dimpled infant's breast.

For many years I walked the earth forlorn,
Seeking, with sighs, a kindred soul to find;
Sometimes my heart, deceived by specious show,
The delicate light tendrils of her love
Flung round a worthless object, as a vine

Might clasp some withered tree, or cling to one
That fed its veins with venom-tainted sap.
But now there is a loving heart that beats
Harmoniously with mine—with mine it thrills
With sudden rush of joy, or sheds sweet tears
Over the Poet's consecrated page;
And not a fiery hope, or passion strong;
No glory-tinted dream, or hope sublime,
Has swept my breast that has not passed o'er his!

Father, I thank thee for his love!—For theirs
That form a sacred chain of linkéd hearts,
Binding my captive will to yonder home
Whose casement beams a welcome to me now.

How luminous the firmament to-night
Gleams through the rarified and frosty air—
One more rapt look, and then, good-night, ye Orbs!
Oh! stars! ye keen-eyed sentinels that guard
The outer wall of Heaven's eternal court,
If aught of ill has mingled with my thoughts,
As I have mused along my lonely walk,
Let them not pass the sapphire battlements,
And speed their way before the Throne of God,
But drive them back to earth to die unbreathed
In the deep, silent caverns of my heart.

The Farewell.

EDMUND, thou wouldst have me sing thee
  Something ere thou leavest my side ;
Little song—for dear remembrance— •
   I have tried !
But my heart is far too heavy,
  And my voice too full of sighs,
And affection's fount up-springing
   Dims mine eyes !
Thou must take these things for tokens—
  Take them in the place of song ;
Some day when poetic pulses
   Beat more strong,
And the tide comes gushing, gushing
  From fond Memory's silent cell,
I a song may send thee, Edmund,
  Worthy in thy soul to dwell ;
  Song shall bind thee as a spell.

Bind thee to the ancient homestead
  Thou hast blessed, too short a time,
With the brightness of thy presence ;
   And the chime
Of the rich, harmonious music
  Springing from thy youthful breast,
Where no sigh of sin or sorrow
   Claims a rest !
Bind thee to the hearts now saddened ;
  To the eyes bedimmed with tears ;
Loving eyes, henceforth must track thy
   Coming years ;

Loving hearts, would shield thee ever
From all sorrow—from all sin ;
Loving hands, a wreath of glory
Weaving for thyself to win ;
Knowing *thee* so strong within !

Ah ! already on my spirit
Falls the shadow of a woe,
As I mark the wingéd hours
Come and go ;
When I think to-morrow takes thee
From our home, *not hearts*, away,
No—those silent spirit chambers
Shall for aye
Hold the love to them entrusted,
Hold the memory of the joy ;
Fling sweet incense from their altars
O'er thee, boy !
Go—no song of mine shall waken
Gloomy echoes on thy way ;
By Love's holy star enlightened—
And its pure effulgent ray
Leading to the perfect day.

For remember Poets ever
Bear a keen prophetic spright ;
They see deeper in the darkness
And the light !
So with eyes fixed on the future
Now I scan thy horoscope
And the great stars stoop and whisper
Words of Hope !

Onward—for thy life expandeth
    To a bright and finished whole;
Onward—urge thy panting spirit
    To the goal!
Rich in youth, in health, in purpose,
    Naught should make thee swerve, or fail;
With thy resolute, bold nature
    Girding thee as coat of mail,
    Onward, man, *thou shalt prevail!*

Sooth *thy poet* is a woman—
    And her heart is full of love,
And the sign upon *that* Ægis
    Is a Dove!
Lo! she bends this pure shield o'er thee—
    Listen to its dove's soft tone:—
Now with garlands of affection
    Would inzone,
But for knowing that all flowers,
    Purely earthly, bloom to die,
Therefore are her eyes uplifted
    To the sky;
And with cool palms fondly resting
    On thy head and glossy hair,
Her true heart above the azure
    Soareth upward with a prayer
    For a blessing on thee, dear.

" Father, to Thy care we leave him,
    Let him very safely lie,
Like a weanéd child in spirit
    'Neath Thine eye!

18

Saviour, in Thy human body
    Seated on the Glory-Throne,
Do Thou claim this youthful brother
       As Thine own!
Spirit pure, from both proceeding,
    God of comfort, joy and love,
Send thy manifold great blessings
      From above,
Let them fall as dews of Hermon,
    On his head, and *in* his breast,
Till he's called to sleep with Jesus
    In a calm and holy rest;
May he waken in the MANSIONS OF THE BLEST!

Springtime.

'Tis Spring—and never did a brighter day
Salute thy rose-bound tresses lovely May!*
All nature smiles—and birds in bower and grove
Pour from their happy bosoms liquid love,
Upon the buoyant air entrancéd floats
The music of those wild impassioned notes;
Young beauty is astir—and I would fling
All sadness from my heart and join her charméd ring.

Fair from my open casement gleams to view
The lakelet with its deep cerulean hue:—
In fancy I am floating on its breast
As on *that* evening, when the glowing west

---

* The opening lines borrowed from Leigh Hunt:
    " 'Tis morn ! and never did a lovelier day
      Salute Ravenna from her leafy bay"—

Lit up its waters, and our tiny boat,
Left to the breezes' pleasure, seemed to float
A fairy shell—or ark where calmly lay
The passions in repose, like weary child at play !

Dost *thou* remember?—I shall e'er retain
The memory of *one* ramble : Blessed rain
Not long before had fallen—and the green
Of the young forest in a silvery sheen
Sparkled, until the god-like sun a ray
Left as a benison to lovely day,
And all the landscape, 'neath a flood of gold,
Lay an illumined page in Nature's volume old !

Now turning from the glory—under trees,
Made musical by evening's sighing breeze,
And arching overhead.   How still and calm !
The silence fell upon our hearts as balm
Upon care-wounded spirits—not a word
In the dim twilight of the wood was heard
To issue from our lips—A loving glance
Had smote too rudely far that deep, soul-mingling
     trance !

Ah ! ne'er again upon that mimic lake—
Nor in the green wood—nor through tangled brake
Fragrant with jasmine, shall we ever stray,
Or float, or dream the passing hours away :
The tale is ended—the sweet poem closed—
The roses withered that so late reposed
Upon my bosom : Still around my room
Thy sere, yet precious garlands shed a faint perfume.

May.

Who is this that cometh
  Tripping up this way?
Glancing in the sunshine,
  Flashing 'neath its ray,
Like a nymph of Faëry
  Airy, bright and gay?

Gaily dance her tresses
  With the wavy air;
Gemmed with dew the roses
  Holding them with care,
In their sweet embraces,
  From her forehead fair!

Quivering in the sunlight,
  Sparkling in the rill,
Glancing on the river
  By the rustic mill;
Her sweet influences
  Doth all Nature fill.

When her sandaled foot-prints
  Brush the dewy mead,
Song-birds' liquid music
  Pour upon her head;
And fresh flowers leap upward
  From their fragrant bed!

Lo! her smile celestial
  Brightens all the air;
Maketh this terrestrial
  Beam an Eden fair;
Emblem of the region
  Where the Angels are!

Maidens! haste to meet her
  Ere she flits away—
Youths! with garlands greet her
  For she will not stay;
Ye shall miss her presence
  From your path some day.

Children! fill your aprons
  With the flowers that spring
Where her sweet breath floateth
  Zephyr on the wing—
And her perfumed darlings
  Back upon her fling.

Wake the slumbering echoes
  With your voices gay,
Till they ring a chorus
  Like sweet bells at play;
Or the merry laughter
  Of some sylvan fay!

Who is this that cometh
  In the silvery sheen
Of the dewy morning;
  Clad in robe of green
Crowned with budding blossoms
  Like a Faëry Queen?

'Tis the fairest daughter
  Of the flowery Spring;
Loveliest of the graces,
  That around her cling;
May—then haste to greet her
  And her praises sing.

Ask of her a blessing
  Ere she hies away ;—
Heart forever keeping
  Joyance of the May ;
Bosom where her flowers
  Bud and bloom for aye.

Quivering in the sunshine ;
  Sparkling in the spray
Of a silvery shower
  Tripping up this way,
Through the arch of Iris
  Comes the merry May.

My Pilgrimage.

BEFORE LEAVING THE "OLD PLANTATION," MAY, 1857.

I.

REACH me my trusty staff and sandal shoon
For I must wend on pilgrimage to-day :—
Or ere the sun sets, or the pensive moon
Comes out to tip the landscape with her ray
I must have traversed all the pleasant way
  Round by the rice-fields to the river's side ;
For certes 'tis the flowery month of May—
And not much longer dare we here abide
Or Death will sweep us hence with his dark restless
    tide !

II.

Out by the back porch ; down the gentle slope,
Pass through the gate and turn toward the right ;
Now give to Fancy ample verge and scope
To range and frolic like a faëry sprite ;
Lo ! this umbrageous foliage doth invite
To linger in the shade that Poets love—
Trust not the sylvan stillness—mellow light—
Pause not to hark the songsters of the grove,
Flinging their fond good-night from waving bough
    above !

III.

Yet by the graveyard pause a little space,
Albeit none but sable forms rest there ;
Do not the willows wave with mournful grace ?
Are not the sleepers quite as much Thy care
Almighty Father ! though of humble sphere,
As those who crumble 'neath sepulchral stone,
Or proud mausoleum—how rich or rare ?
Will not Thy mercy claim them as thine own,
Did not for them, as well, Thy Holy One atone ?

IV.

Here rests that model form tho' bronzed its hue ;
Here sleep those eyes which shone so softly bright ;
How cold the manly heart that beat so true
A note for Heaven ere the veil of night
Fell for a moment o'er his soul and light :—
Yonder a broken-hearted mother sleeps—
Here, where this new-made hillock hides from sight
A drownéd son, an aged father weeps,
While for his blighted youth he midnight vigil keeps !

V.

And many aged souls, ripe Autumn grain,
Have here been garnered from the Winter's cold;
We may not pass them by without the rain
Of feeling dropping on the grass-grown mould;—
O, may they now be happy in the fold
Of the immortal Shepherd! *There we know*,
The angels of the litle ones behold
The Father's visage and in wisdom grow
Meet for th' Eternal light will one day from it flow!

VI.

Onward—and upward, for a tiny mount
Invites the Pilgrim kindly to ascend—
Plant well thy sturdy walking-staff—nor count
The weeds and brambles that together blend
T' impede thy passage; soon the way will end,
And the sweet scene repay thy little toil;
List to the music of the pines that send
Perfume as well to mingle with the spoil
Wind-rifled from the plants bepranking all the soil!

VII.

Behold Mount Kath'rine!—'tis a pleasant spot,
Altho' its fame and history be unknown—
We *will not* call it " Poplar Hill," for not
A vesture of such tree an age has grown
Upon its summit!—twenty years have flown
Since it received the name that now it bears,
Yet doth a thought float round it like a zone
Of starlight from the past—but ah! sad tears
Will mingle with the gleam that rises with those years.

VIII.

Why ruffle up the past! How calmly rest
The watered rice-fields 'neath the sun's good-night!
Scarcely a ripple stirs their glassy breast,
Thus let it be with thine. The road of right,—
Altho' a thousand spectres thee affright,
Looming up in the shadow—travel on,
Soon shall the distant goal appear in sight
Then will vain phantoms of the dark be gone,
And Jesus give the crown His death for thee has won!

IX.

Peace to yon mansion lifting o'er the trees
Its venerable roof, 'neath which repose
Hearts that beat fondly for me—may the breeze,
From whate'er quarter of the heaven it blows
Waft countless blessings to it—scatter woes
And ills from out its precincts. Friendship's rest!
May the fast coming ages but disclose
New virtues of thy rearing! Honor's crest
Wave from the front of those four fledglings of thy nest!

X.

Now with light foot-beat leave the breezy hill—
Passing where soft a water channel glides;
Onward, while birds around thee sweetly trill
Their evening song, and the proud sun-god hides
Behind his purple canopy and bides
His glorious reäwakening: Who is here
In the old mill at work? A tear-drop slides
Adown his cheek the while—cross o'er and cheer
With word from God's own Book we know he keepeth
near.
19

XI.

Now on with quick accelerated tread—
Dark hastens on apace—the night-birds wail;
The bright stars look from their celestial bed
And sanctify the scene!   Soft vesper gale
Plays musically sweet as from the rail
Of the old bridge, I lean to hear it sigh
Among the lithe reeds—like an o'er sad tale
Told to the chime of some old minstrelsy,
While silver drops rain down from gentle Beauty's eye!

XII.

Old bridge! how many recollections cling
To thee and thy surroundings?   Here of yore
A boy friend would soar-up on buoyant wing,
As a glad bird, and streams of classic lore
Pour from his heart!   Last Sabbath eve thy shore
I pressed with one, how holy, silver tide
Rolling beneath these planks!   Thy water bore
Our spirits onward, in its gentle glide
Far pass the verge of Time, or Jordan's gloomy side!

XIII.

Pure as the ideal of a poet's soul,
Or lily-cup with dew-drops fed from Heaven;
Thy body formed of clear ethereal mould
In early youth to God, by Faith was given;
Like Samuel, thou waitest morn and even
Upon Jehovah!   And perchance hast heard
His voice at midnight calling, nor hast striven
To banish it thine heart.   That MIGHTY LORD,
Thou offerest to thy flock in his life-giving WORD.

XIV.

E'en as the flowers of which you spoke that eve,
Blooming in desert place for God alone;
So the calm beauty of your life you weave
In these secluded wilds—our gifted one!
Our well-beloved Pastor!   In this zone,*
This little zone 'twixt parallel of light
And beauty beaming, be your Shepherd Throne
Forever rooted; from its modest height
Send forth the perfect Law to rule our hearts aright.

XV.

Home through the Orchard, sung in early strain,
The day is spent—Yet in this cot awhile
I must abide with one in age and pain,
Hand the low stool, and quick the pine-knots pile
That light may reach the page; I must beguile
This weary soul from Earth.   What better end
To my calm pilgrim ramble than the smile
Playing around thy mouth, my aged friend,
While in the Saviour's praise our mutual voices blend!

---

*Rev. W. B. W. Howe, now Rector of St. Philip's Church,
Charleston.

A Portrait from Memory.

Oh! for the Poet's power,
Or Limner's art, this hour,
To make thee start all life-like forth to view;
Thy locks of golden brown,
So wildly streaming down;
And eyes, whose every change shot beams of beauty
new!

Perfect in manly grace;
No jarring line we trace:
When in the game of Fence, with skilful art,
Thy lithe foil's airy play,
And eyes keen focal ray,
Alike had power to pierce the foe or gazer's heart.

To me thou art brighter far
Than morn or evening star,
Or young Apollo beaming forth the light!
More lovely than that flower
Couched in aerial bower
That tempted Dian's self from her celestial height!

Even that simple wand
So often in thine hand
Seemed but to add to thy mysterious power;
Had it some weird-like charm?
Some wizard-might to harm?
Was't blessed, beneath the moon, in Sybil's lonely
bower?

Ah me! there was a spell—
From *it* or *thee* that fell
Upon my heart, and thrilled it into song;
And still it gives a sound,
As when the wild wind's round
Strike from Æolian wires, echoes deep and strong!

A Valentine.

FOR E. M. G.

To-morrow is St. Valentine,
And I would send to thee
A greeting from my distant home
By the sparkling, green-robed sea;
I'm sitting by the lattice high,
My seat in summer hours,
To catch the fitful breezes' play,
And the perfume of the flowers.

But not to hail old Valentine,
The jocund Saint of Love,
Would I borrow now the downy wing
Of the low-voiced carrier dove;
It is no light and airy lay
His pinion soon must bear,
Such freight thy blue-eyed maiden may
Confide unto his care.

But I a note of high resolve
Would strike from out my lyre,
A note to rouse thy manly heart,
To 'wake its latent fire:

For 'neath thy cold and calm extern
   Slumbers volcanic flame
Shall burst, and bring before the world,
   For good or ill, thy name!

Awake! and consecrate the morn—
   The birth-morn of thy sire—
With every high and holy vow,
   With every pure desire!
Be all thy sister's loving heart
   Would have her darling prove;
Fulfil thy father's soaring hope,
   Thy mother's yearning love.

Slumbering Poesy.

I.

Once more my spirit in the magic round
Of Fancy has been sporting; building slight
Ærial castles upon Faëry ground,
Filled with ideal beauty! What delight!
Methought my path had been forsaken quite
By all such airy visions, ne'er again
To flit before me in their beauty bright,
And garments woven of the glorious grain
Fair shining in the arc that cometh after rain!

II.

For as a wood-nymph in a shady grot,
Impervious to the Sun's reviving ray,
Lies calmly slumbering while around the spot
The wild-birds carol and the breezes play;

Where scarcely Pan himself might find the way
Of entrance—tho' perchance a laughing Faun
With ivy-crownèd forehead there may stray,
Brushing the silver dew at streak of dawn
Just ere the morning star her radiance has withdrawn!

III.

So in my bosom gentle Poësy
Lay sleeping as if naught might break her trance;
No sigh her bosom stirred to prophesy—
No holy rapture kindled her soft glance—
No thought ecstatic caused her to advance
With springing feet toward Parnassus dread,
And from Castalia's classic stream perchance
Quaff inspiration—and contented tread
Beneath the sacred leaves have crowned the poet's
    head!

IV.

I deemed thee dead—but lo! the infant breath
Of Spring came floating o'er thy slumbering eyes,
Rich with the perfume of the flowery heath,
And warm with sunny heat from azure skies;
It caused thee *stir*—but could not make thee *rise*—
That power to Love o'er Nature's self was given,
His magic touch through all thy body flies
A living light-flash! Thy long trance is riven
And on exultant wing thou soarst from Earth to Heaven!

V.

O Love! O Friendship! or by whate'er name
Is named the passion that has roused my heart,
Still work thou in that deep recess; inflame
All my dull nature by thy mighty art;—

Yet may suspicion of the truth ne'er dart
In the Magician's breast! All hail the gift!
Albeit possession causes many a smart
Of keenest anguish—for the muse can lift
Our souls above the sea where our wrecked blessings
    drift.

VI.

Spirit of Inspiration! Vision bright!
Now standing by my timid Poësy;
May she enfold thee in her arms of white?
Or will thine essence fade before her eye
As evanescent as a gentle sigh
Wafted from woman's heart? A happy dream?
A note Æolian flitting wildly by?—
In transitory glory dost thou beam?
Or wilt thou, Faëry Sprite, accompany life's stream?

VII.

Say wilt thou lead her with thy gentle hand
Along the flowery steepness of the hill,
Until she views from far the Poet band
Sitting in God-like beauty, calm and still,
Each on his star-lit throne! To list the trill
Of Phœbus' lyre floating down the wind,
Whilst every august muse to her sweet will
Tempers the music—and in every mind
Apollo's heavenly notes responsive echoes find!

VIII.

Thou fadest upon my vision—and art gone!
And my sad muse drops down on languid wing,
And droops to her old covert, sick—forlorn—
Never to mount aloft and freely sing,

Unless once more the life-dispensing Spring,
And that far greater power of Love unite
Their genial essence, and around her fling
Their magic spell resistless; Then in might
She will again arise and take her Heavenward flight!

Love.

DEAR one, seekest thou to know
If my heart-blood's ruby flow,
And its altar's burning glow
   Are for thee alone?

Listen to the tale I'll tell—
Thou hast bound me in a spell;
Flowery fetters are they?   Well
   Still I am not free.

By the paleness, or the flush
O'er my conscious cheeks that rush;
By my heart's mysterious hush—
   Know thou art beloved.

By the trembling of my frame
When thy well-belovéd name
Unexpected to me came,
   Know thou art adored.

By my fond heart's rapid beat
When I catch thine accents sweet;
Or thy smiling eyelids greet
   My approaching form.

By the thrill which through my breast
Rushes when my hand is prest
By thy hand—the truth's confest
  That I love thee well.

Scarce these tell-tale eyes of mine
Dare I to uplift to thine,
Ere the lids I quick decline
  Lest they should betray.

By my spirit's varying flow
Swelling high—then ebbing low ;
By my piteous sighs of woe
  Know thou art beloved.

Keen the anguish of my heart
When from thee I'm forced to part,
By this token know thou art
  Treasured in my soul.

By the jealous fire that burns
In my bosom's secret urns
When I fear *thy* spirit turns
  To another maid.

By the blessings that I pour,
From my heart's exhaustless store,
On the one whom I adore
  Know thou art beloved.

Know thou art beloved !   My breast
Holds *that secret* unconfest
And I solemnly attest
  There it shall abide.

Like the perfumed lamps that burned
Where the dead, to dust returned,
Lay in antique tombs inurned—
      Glowing in my heart!

But perhaps when Time has flown
And we meet before the Throne,
There the secret may be known
      Of my loving breast!

L'Adieu.

AH! many weeks must pass away,
  And many months perchance,
Ere I thy witching smile shall see
  Or, meet thy brilliant glance—
Thy brilliant glance that as a flash
  Of summer, lightning plays,
Throwing a halo round the close
  Of Life's declining days!

Thy smile! Oh! it has power to wake
  Within my bosom's close,
The slumbering hope that in it lies
  As sunbeams 'wake the Rose.
As sunbeams 'wake the sleeping Rose
  Within her fragrant bower,
And turn to gems of sparkling light
  The sad-night's dewy shower!

Thy word—thy softly whispered word,
  Floats as a zephyr light
Upon my spirit's troubled tide
  As breezes of the night—

As breezes of the starry night
  Play o'er the heaving sea,
On which the fairy moonbeams dance
  In airy, sportive glee!

Thy smile, thy glance, thy whispered word.
  Will they be garnered all,
Until upon my startled ear
  Thy well-known footsteps fall?
Or, wilt thou cast those precious gifts
  Among the light and gay,
All heedless of the loving heart
  That's breaking far away?

The Meeting.

WE met—'twas after many years
  Of absence and of pain,
And I had thought that we on Earth
  Should never meet again:
We met—where we were wont to meet
  When life was all a dream,
And the glad moments glided by
  Bright as a woodland stream.

Days when we decked our bowers of joy
  With fragrant summer flowers,
And all the tears our young eyes wept
  Were sweet refreshing showers—
Were sweet refreshing shower-drops shed
  Upon the germs of Hope,
That in our youthful bosoms gleamed,
  Fair, budding heliotrope!

We met—and the long buried past
  Came sweeping o'er my soul
As when the fierce Autumnal blast
  Breaks from the Northern Pole,
And stirreth in his rude career
  The buds and flowers that lie
Withered upon the garden beds,—
  On wild-wing rushing by!

Thus all the youthful hopes that slept
  Within my heart profound,
Were by a blast from Memory's breath
  Whirled wildly round and round
All sere and withered—yet the sight
  Of those long perished flowers
Sufficed a secret sigh to swell
  O'er long-forgotten hours!

I felt my bosom cease to beat;
  I felt my visage pale;
I felt a coldness all within
  As life itself would fail!
Then silently I breathed a prayer
  To vestal, maiden Pride,
To help me in that needful hour
  My foolish fear to hide.

It is not that I love thee still—
  Oh, no! that day is past;
Thou canst not now recall the gem
  Thy ruthless folly cast
Into the Ocean of Despair,
  —Now many years agone—
To sink beneath its booming tide
  As 'twere a worthless stone!

No—no; thy smile has lost its charm—
   Yet many things combine,
Of late the tendrils of sad thought
   Around the past to twine;
One has been with us who was here
   In those bright hours of joy;—
And, when we met, we gazed upon
   Another's darling boy!

Oh no!—not Love—It is not Love
   That moves my spirit so,
Yet some time o'er the vanished past
   Fond memory's tears must flow!
Not Love—Oh! I have done with Love!
   Nor shall a floweret more
From the false Gardens of the Past
   Gleam in my bosom's core!

Sonnet.

TO MRS. A. B. S., OF COLUMBIA, S. C., ON DECLINING AN INVITA-
TION TO ACCOMPANY HER TO ALABAMA.

FAREWELL kind friend, I may not go with thee—
   But I shall follow on the wing of prayer,
   And hover round and bless thee *even there*
Amid the happy circle, that with free
Light-hearted mirth, and hospitable glee,
   Shall hail thine advent, and instate with care,
   Thee, venerable Mother, in the chair
Kept sacred for thy use. Then think of me,
Nor let the vision of my solemn face,

Throw gloom upon the gladness—but mine eye
Beam, as it ever does when thou art nigh,
And tell of true affection ; in it trace
My heart's deep love which Time shall ne'er efface,
And God shall bless in worlds beyond the sky.

Sonnet.

TO MARY F.

PURE as a moonbeam sleeping on the sea ;
Or playing in the chalice of a flower,
In some romantic Fairy-cultured bower,
Seems thy sweet maiden presence unto me
With its soft light, and holy witchery
Of Christian graces ; the peculiar dower
Of stern Affliction, who in Life's young hour
Put out the Sun and left sad night to thee,—
Yet not a night of darkness and of gloom,—
Bright solemn stars look from its deep blue sky ;
And silvery moonbeams ripple and illume
Thy path else dreary—and allure thine eye
To where *thy friend* amid perpetual bloom,
Awaits thy coming in the realm on high.

The Dreamer.

MAIDEN of the pensive air,
Thoughtful brow and visage fair,
Wherefore hast thou left thy home
In these solemn woods to roam?
On this flowery bank to rest,
When the sun toward the west
Scarce his burning eye has cast,
Or his noontide journey past?

Know'st thou not that duties wait
Clustering round the cottage gate?
Where thy aged mother sighs,
There thy woman's mission lies;
Mortal man must gain his bread
By the labor of the head,
Or the sweat upon his brow—
Dreamer, wake to duty now!

Wouldst thou be content to glide
Down Life's deep and rapid tide,
Like a blossom from its spray
By the tempest swept away,
Ere the germ of life was warmed—
Ere the precious fruit was formed—
To be cast, thy voyage o'er,
Worthless on th' eternal shore?

Wherefore hast thou left thy rest,
In thy soft and sheltered nest
By the altar's side, and flown
Birdlike to the woods alone?

Here thy plaintive lays to trill
By some sweetly murmuring rill,
Rather than attune thy throat
To the Temple's solemn note?

Dreamer, it will be too late
When thou stand'st before the gate,
And high battlements of Heaven;
Then this answer will be given
To thy oft repeated knocks,
Though the very portal rocks
'Neath the heavy blows—" Depart
Jesus knows not who thou art."

Wake then Dreamer, and thy rest
Seek upon the Saviour's breast;
With his dove-like flock abide
In the cleft Rocks rugged side,
Till the howling wintry blast—
Till the weary night is past—
And sweet flowers of Spring appear
To bloom through Love's eternal year.

A Farewell to the Old Homestead.

ALAS! I must leave on the morrow this, the dear dome
of affection—
The home of my heart and my hope, where my joys
and my sorrows have centered.
Farewell, it is hard to quit thee and all thy surroundings,
Venerable homestead! where erst in innocent childhood I sported.
20

'Twas here, in the springtime of life, my heart first
    opened its petals,
And shed the rich perfume of love o'er a youthful
    and careless companion;
Here when the sunlight of May had called forth each
    wonderful blossom
That springs from the soil of the heart, I culled me the
    rarest and fairest,
And scattered them all in the path of one, how un-
    worthy the treasure;
Like a cup that ever is full, my heart poured forth her
    rich nectar,
But he cared not to drink of its sweets, and it flowed
    back the waters of Marah.
So when June came on in her strength, her sunlight,
    her flush, and her fever,
I put forth my hand and seized the rosy garland of
    Pleasure;
The thorns entered deep in my flesh, and red blood,
    rolled down my white fingers.
Methought I would choose me a friend, they are said
    to be better than kindred;
But my friend he mistook my word—the iron entered
    my bosom.
Next I essayed me to sweep the golden harp of the
    Muses,
Trembling, my hand 'woke a sound that passed away
    into—Oblivion.
Since Love, the pure dew from the sky that falls and
    refreshes the spirit,
And Pleasure, and Friendship and Song, had every one
    caus'd disappointment—
Then said I " Give me my staff and the amice cloak of
    the pilgrim,

I will turn my face to the East, and make for the city
    of Sion ;"
But the way it is lonely and drear, and darksome, and
    flickers
The light that should lighten my steps, and beam on
    the pillar of Ezel :
Yea, have I prayed with the sick ; yea, have I wept
    with the straying ;
Yet fear I shall never attain where the angels in glory
    are singing !
Here have I joyed and rejoiced ; here have I wept and
    lamented
Through Life's early Spring and its Summer ; year by
    year as I came,
Renewing heart-joy and heart-sorrow. And now in the
    Autumn
Still cling, O homestead beloved ! to thy bosom ; when
    Winter's chill breath
Recalls from afar the sad-hearted exiles, wide open
    thine arms to receive,
And embraced let me lie, in life or in death, on thy
    bosom.
    May 16th, 1858.

To My Godson, T. B. P., in England.

LITTLE Godson, far away
    O'er the heaving billow,
Nightly ere my head I lay
    On my downy pillow,
I commend thee to the care
Of the God who heareth prayer,
Beg Him on His breast to bear
    And protect thee ever.

On the breast of Jesus laid,
   Nestle close, lie soft and still,
Of thy foes be not afraid,
   He will guard from ill;
Calmly look up in His face,
There the lines of mercy trace;
Note the beam of Heavenly Grace
   Raying on thee ever.

Listen to the cooing note
   Of the Spirit-Dove,
On the pleasant air afloat,
   Wooing thee to love!
When my prayers are weak and vain,
And thy childish accents fain
Would mount up, to earth again,
   Beaten down by sin—

He takes up our feeble cry,
   Bears it on his wing
Where the cherubs wheel and fly, '
   In a golden ring,
Round Jehovah's cloud-wrapt throne,
There with earnest, pitying moan
Pleads for us before the One
   Died our life to win!

Listen! all around thee there,
   In the Mother Land,
Mystic music on thine ear
   Welleth sweet and grand;
Every venerable pile,
Ruin hoar, and haunted aisle,
Echoes lend to reconcile
   Sinners to The Slain!

Venerate her church, my child,
  Spring from whence our own,
In this far-off western wild,
  From a rill has grown
To a river flowing free,
To the vast, eternal sea,
In whose saving billows we
  Have been cleansed from stain.

When upon the sparkling sands
  With thy Mother dear,
Or with romping, boyish bands
  Drinking English air—
Think of one who evermore
Longeth for her sea-girt shore;
Loveth her blessed ancient lore,
  And her poet band.

O that I could wing my flight
  O'er the sounding billow,
To the Isle, my dream by night,
  When, on downy pillow,
I escape from every care
Hedging me around, and there
With my friend, and Godson dear,
  Press the British strand.

Love Among the Roses.

In the springtime 'mong the roses
  Met I Love—he said to me,
" Row a little down the river
  And a vision you shall see,
Of a maiden bright and joyous,
  Not a blonde—but richly hued,
Telling that her mantling blushes
  Come of noble Southern blood."

Thrilling there among the roses,
  Said I to the Elfin Sprite,
(Smiling archly mid the flowers ;
  Quivering his pinions light)—
" But perchance the pretty maiden
  Coyly should avert her head,
Wildly then my heart would flutter
  With a strange, mysterious dread."

" Fearing that the word decisive,
  Trembling on her ruby lip,
Might be *one* the budding blossoms
  Of my Spring of Life to nip ;
Better then that I had never
  Launched my boat upon the stream,
Dropping downward to the maiden
  In a sweet, delicious dream.

" Floating—with the mystic influence
  Of the season on my soul ;
Dreamily—yet all in earnest,
  Bowing to its sweet control :

Godlike Love! thy power is mighty,
  Filling Earth, and Air, and Tide—
Tell me—shall I dare to woo her
  To become mine own—my bride?"

Then he shook his golden pinions,
  Till the garden glowed with light,
Spread them forth, and soaring upward
  Vanished in the azure height;
Hear the note he dropped to earthward
  As he fanned the fragrant air,
"Never heart of timid lover
  Won the love of maiden fair!"

And I took his words for comfort—
  Prophesy of happy end;
And I dropped adown the river
  To my shy, awaiting friend;
There she sat beneath the shimmer
  Of the trees' protecting shade;
And before the stars had risen
  I had won the blushing maid.

Strawberry Ferry.

A BALLAD.

Not a May Day in the forest—
  But a May Day on the flood,
Rocking for three mortal hours,
  It was not *so very good;*
Rocking for three mortal hours,
  On a rough, unruly tide,
Toiling, poling, sweating, fretting,
  For to reach the other side.

Very loath the lazy freedmen
　Were to push us from the shore,
Until "Johnny" kindly told them
　He would help to put us o'er;
Stripping to the work in earnest,—
　Poling up against the stream,
Wind and tide both set against us—
　This was no "delicious dream."

At the fish-trap we were boarded
　By two travellers, who would,
Like ourselves, have crossed the river
　By the ferry—if they could;
One a friend with whom in girlhood
　I had frolicked many a day,
In the big house, now a ruin,
　That we passed upon the way.

As the polers toiled, we chatted
　Pleasantly, to pass the time,
Of the days long gone—and ever,
　When the world was in its prime;
When we fancied Time would never
　Row us o'er Life's sunny stream,
To the far-off Land of Shadow,
　Where *the past* becomes a dream.

Now the flat had crossed the river,
　And the haven seemed at hand,
Vain the hope, alas! as ever,
　We were not to reach the land,
Wearied out, our two companions,
　Hailed a "darkie" paddling o'er,
Ventured in his skiff—and after
　Sundry efforts, made the shore.

Then *we* drifted back to landward,
    Far below the Ferry slip;
Ran aground—and sighed for patience
    To endure our pleasant trip;
Then methought, in place of sighing,
    And to charm the tyrant Time,
I would set our May Day frolic
    To a rough and rugged chime.

Dreamily the snowy "Cloudland"
    Floated on the azure sky;
While the green verge of the river
    Lay refreshing to the eye;
But nor "cloudland" in its beauty,
    Nor the tree-tops shivering sheen,
Could beguile the weary waiting,
    Or the heart from fretting wean.

Rocked the flat—the brown wave sparkled
    'Neath the May sun's brilliant glow,
While the wind dashed up the cooling
    Spray-drops to my fevered brow;
Far above in the pure ether
    Flew the buzzards—circling round
Gracefully—then sweeping downward
    To their prey upon the ground.

Cheerfully my young companion
    Took the tedious waiting time,
For his heart made sweeter music
    Than my rough, unpolished rhyme;
Singing, softly, to a maiden,
    Love's bewitching roundelay;
Weaving visionary garlands
    For his chosen Queen of May.

Hurrah! see the tide is turning!
   Three o'clock!—and now once more
We are moving—onward—upward,
   Slowly by the pebbly shore;
Gnarled and knotted roots and branches
   Rest upon their marly bed;
While the song-birds shower music
   From the tree-tops overhead.

Lo! again the little "dug-out"
   Dancing lightly on the tide,
Paddled by the two companions,
   Crosses to the Homeward side;
To the side I loved in gladness
   In my May Day's happy light;
To the side I love in sadness
   Now my May has suffered blight.

In the Ferry-boat, May Day, 1867.

www.ingramcontent.com/pod-product-compliance
Lightning Source LLC
Chambersburg PA
CBHW020851270326
41928CB00006B/647